BEFORE YOUR VERY EYES

Before your very eyes

Arthur Askey

THE WOBURN PRESS

First published
in Great Britain in 1975 by
THE WOBURN PRESS
67 Great Russell Street,
London WC1B 3BT

ISBN 0 7130 0134 8

Printed in Great Britain by
Butler & Tanner Ltd, Frome and London

Contents

	Preface	13
1	Small Beginnings	15
2	Halcyon Days	25
3	A Little Caution	36
4	Nothing Like a Dame	50
5	Top of the Poll	59
6	Anthea's Début	71
7	Birth of *Band Waggon*	83
8	The Bee's Knees	93
9	*Waggon* Goes to War	103
10	Looking up to Society	118
11	Not Shaw about Agate	134
12	By Royal Appointment	142
13	Big Down Under	152
14	Before Your Very Eyes	163
15	Behind the Heart	176
	Postscript	190

Illustrations

Following page 16:

    With portrait by John Bratby
    My mother, Betsy Bowden Askey
    My father, Samuel Askey
    Me, age two
    Five years old and about to start school
    My first stage appearance in *Jan of Windmill Land*
    As a choir boy
    My school group at the Liverpool Institute
    Before the dance, with best friend Billy Bird
    Starting work at Liverpool Corporation
    Dad, Rene, Mother and me, on our last holiday at Rhyl

Following page 32:

    In the Welch Regiment at Kinmel Camp, 1918
    A vocal recital by Private A. Askey
    The special girl in my life
    Our football group: we won, 2–1
    Members of *Song Salad* at Ventnor
    In pierrot costume for *The Filberts*
    My first professional photograph

Following page 48:

    The first Dame, in pantomime at Southsea – influenced
        by Dan Leno
    May's debut with *Song Salad*
    Fred Wildon's Margate Entertainers
    Powis Pinder's *Sunshine Company* at Shanklin
    On stage at Shanklin
    With Charlie Harrison in *Babes in the Wood*, Nottingham,
        1933

Following page 48:

About to sing *The Bee*
King of the Masonics
23 March 1925: May and Arthur Askey, with family
  and friends
With Mother and May at Margate, 1929
Left holding the baby!
May, Mother, Anthea, Dad and me, on the beach at
  Shanklin

Following page 64:

The Austin 16 and family, 1936
The Hudson at Hammersmith, 1939
The Mercedes, more recently
The *Band Waggon* gang
With Lewis the goat
Pioneer days on radio, teaching Julie Andrews a thing or
  two
Stinker and Big at the top of Broadcasting House
The first and only edition of Arthur Askey's Annual, 1939
My weekly spot in *Radio Fun*

Following page 80:

On stage with Dickie Murdoch
The Palladium programme, 1939
From the *Band Waggon* film: Stinker taking me off
In *Jack and Jill* at the Palace Theatre, London, with Eddie
  Gray
Charley's 'Big-hearted' Aunt
At Scapa Flow with Jack Hylton and Sir Bruce Fraser
Typical wartime performance at the Nuffield Centre

Following page 96:

The Love Racket
In *Follow the Girls*, 1945
  A clutch of comics: Stan Laurel, Sid Field, Val Parnell,
    Danny Kaye, and me

Following page 96:

Rehearsing a Royal Command Performance
The Command Performance that never was: George (Liberace's brother), Max Bygraves, Liberace, me and Jimmy Wheeler, 1956
Meeting her Majesty the Queen and Prince Philip, at the Command Performance, Blackpool, 1955
Approaching New York
In New York, with Olsen and Johnson

Following page 144:

My favourite panto role: 'Buttons' in *Cinderella*
As Prince Ras Monolulu in *The Kid from Stratford*
In *Babes in the Wood*, at the Palladium, 1965
Meeting Sir Robert Menzies at the Tivoli, Melbourne
With Aneurin Bevan and his wife Jenny Lee, at the opening night of *Bet Your Life*, 1951
Sold to Jack Hylton, 1952
With Hancock in the early days of Television
Causing a disturbance at Highbury
Before your very eyes . . . Sabrina
The finishing touches at Madame Tussauds: Mac Hobley looks on
Anthea and Bill, 2 March 1956
Anthea's coming of age with Gracie Fields

Following page 160:

Presenting Gold Disc to Paul and Linda McCartney
This is your life
Fifty years in show biz with Danny La Rue, Roger Moore, Jimmy Edwards, Eric Morecambe and Ernie Wise
With Prince Charles and Eric Morecambe at the Goon Show Scripts launching
With Anthea, Bill, and Grandchildren

Photo Acknowledgements:

Associated British Picture Corporation Ltd; Associated Press Ltd; BBC; Blackpool Gazette & Herald Ltd; British Railways Board; Michael Busselle; Gainsborough Films Ltd; George J. Keen, Staines; Keystone Press Agency Ltd; London Express News and Feature Services; Doug McKenzie Photographic Services Ltd; Michael Putland; Syndication International Ltd; Thames TV Ltd.

TOO HOOM IT MAY CONSERN —
i HAVE BIN CUMISHIONED 2 RITE THE
TAIL OF MI LIFE AT THIS POYNT IN
TIME AS i HAVE JUST COMPLEATED
50 YEERS IN SHOW-BIZ. UNLIKE MOST
THREATICAL BIOGRAFFIES i ROTE THIS ORL
BUY MISELF — NO "GOASTIN" OR "ASISTED BUY"
RUBISH. HAS U NO, MOST OF MI KONTEMPERIES
KAN'T EVEN SPEL KAT. iF i DO MAKE AN
OKKAZIONAL ERRER — THE GENTILMAN FROM
THE PUBLISHARES SEZ HE'LL TAKE OVER.
IN THE MEANTIME, URE IN FOUR A
BLUDDY GUD REED.

Preface

First of all, what to call the book. I have used so many catchphrases through the years – 'Hello, playmates', 'I thank you', 'Before your very eyes', etc. – even 'Big-hearted Author' might be an idea. My daughter Anthea suggested as a title 'Is he as funny at home?' (which she is constantly asked), but there might be those among you who would say, 'Is he funny anywhere?'! Anyway, if you look on the cover of the book, you will see which title was decided upon.

I have written this book 'off the top of my head', with no reference books or diaries whatsoever. (You can tell I have a good memory by my jokes.) The only help I have had is from my press-cutting books. These were kept by my mother in my early days and anything that was at all critical about me was immediately consigned to the waste-paper basket. So my early life in show business would appear to be one long success story!

Before starting to write this biography, I paid a sentimental journey to Liverpool to try and revive old memories of my early years. I naturally went to see the house where I was born. They've got a plaque on the wall that tells the whole romantic legend in one word—'Condemned'!

Before getting 'stuck in' to the Askey Saga, I would like to thank my sister Rene for deciphering my scrawl and typing all the 80,000 words. (This will save me paying her!) Also my daughter Anthea for reminding me of the various episodes in my life, and the gentleman from the publishers, for his advice and correcting the few spelling mistakes I might have made. Also, for deleting the more lurid and purple passages of my private life which would have made David Niven's *The Moon's a Balloon* read like *Little Women*!

Most of all, I would like to thank the great British public for keeping me in regular employment for fifty years. No matter how good one's agent is, or how friendly one is with impresarios or the press, it is the audiences – whether stage, radio, television, or screen – who are the eventual judges and therefore, your employers. So to you, Playmates, I say a sincere 'Aythangyow'! Putting up with me all these years proves that Abraham Lincoln was wrong: you *can* fool all the people – all of the time!

So now, to quote a popular song of today, 'Where do I begin?' The answer lies in an equally popular song, sung by Julie Andrews:

> Let's start at the very beginning –
> A very good place to start.

I was born in a basket of dirty tights
In a broken-down theatre in Crewe,
My Dad was a red-nosed comedian,
My Mother was Danny La Rue.

IT DOESN'T get a laugh on the stage either! And, of course, it's not true – I was actually born in The Holy Land! This was the name given to a small area in the dockland of Liverpool, which consisted of streets named David, Jacob, Isaac, and Moses. In the front bedroom of 29 Moses Street, on 6 June 1900, was born to Samuel and Betsy (née Bowden) Askey the gift of a son. There is no plaque on the wall of the house to commemorate this great event – yet!

When I was six months old, either on account of complaints from the neighbours, or because the family wished to better themselves, we moved to a rather *nicer* district. Naturally, I did not give them any help with the handcart, but we moved into 90 Rosslyn Street: three-up, two-down, bathroom, and two loos (one outside).

I cannot remember too much about my very early years. After

all, it was a long time ago. But I do remember my paternal grand-
father and grandmother. Grandad was a typical Liverpool docker:
I think I saw him only once when he was sober, and obviously not
himself. My grandma used to call occasionally for a 'touch', but
got short shrift from my mother. My mother had two brothers:
Arthur (whom I am named after – Arthur Bowden Askey), and
Edward, known as Ned. Ned was quite a character and lived with
us for a short time. He had a habit of reading aloud from the newspaper, but as he was not much of a scholar he would just pause
when he came to a long word and say 'Manchester'. For example,
'The coroner brought in a verdict of . . . "Manchester",' sort of
thing.

Uncle Arthur married Auntie Barbara, who came from Oswald-
thwistle, and it was she who first taught me little songs and nursery
rhymes, which probably laid the foundations of the genius to come!
In addition to the nursery rhymes, I also learned what I term my
father's 'Bathroom Ballads'. Every morning while washing and
shaving he would sing songs from a large repertoire ranging from
'When I survey the Wondrous Cross' to 'Boiled Beef and Carrots'.

Rosslyn Street was in the Parish of St Michael's-in-the-Hamlet,
and it was the feeling and the changing moods of this area that became engraved on my imagination. The river Mersey flowed past
at the end of the street, and in the distance were the Welsh mountains, which could be clearly seen when it was going to rain. Another
certain sign of rain was the croaky whistle of the trains on the Great
Central Railway which ran between Liverpool and Manchester.
The railway line was almost on the banks of the Mersey, running
along the Cast Iron shore, and I was to use our local station, St
Michael's, constantly when, in 1911, I went to the Liverpool Institute High School for Boys, and later when I was a clerk in the
Education Office.

Between the railway and the river was a private recreation ground,
known affectionately as 'The Crick' – short for cricket field. I was
to spend many happy hours there during my first twenty years.
For an annual fee of five bob (twenty-five pence to younger readers)
you were given a key which entitled you to enter the ground where
there were bowling greens, half a dozen tennis courts, and a
cricket pitch. Even grassy slopes were provided for us kids to play

With portrait by John Bratby

Upper Left: My mother, Betsy Bowden Askey.
Upper Right: My father, Samuel Askey.
Lower Left: Me, age two. *Lower Right:* Five years old and about to start school.

My school group at the Liverpool Institute.

Below: Before the dance, with best friend Billy Bird.
Right: Starting work at Liverpool Corporation.
Bottom: Dad, Rene, Mother and me, on our last holiday at Rhyl.

roly-poly down to the wall that kept the 'buckoes' out. We often had the odd stone thrown at us from the rough types on the shore, not that we didn't reply, or even start it, on occasion. Shades of Belfast. With its strong Catholic population and the prejudices, there was always a slight undercurrent of unrest in Liverpool. My mother, a staunch Wesleyan, would clip my ear if she found me playing with 'that Catholic boy from next door'. Ironically I am certain that my ancestors on my father's side came from Ireland. The quick temper, the love of music, and the fiery-red hair (I was always Rusty, Ginger, or Coppernob at school) were distinct characteristics in both my father and me. My mother was more sedate, coming from Knutsford in Cheshire.

When I started at St Michael's Council School I was five and already finding my aunt's nursery rhymes and my father's ballads helping me towards success. I was soon quite a teacher's pet, singing and showing off in front of the class. However, all my young social life was really centred around the church: morning and evening services on Sunday, with Sunday School in the afternoon; Band of Hope on Monday; Scripture Union on Tuesday; choir practice on Wednesday; rehearsals for the church concert on Thursday; more choir practice on Friday. Even on Saturday there would usually be a garden fête, or a bazaar connected with the church. No wonder that for a long time I wanted to take Holy Orders – and I don't mean darning socks!

I started in the choir as a probationer at threepence a month. You had to wait for one of the choristers' voices to break before you got your chance. Mine came and it was the tallest boy in the choir who had to leave, so I got his cassock and surplice. To fit 'Titch' Askey they had to be turned up, and the tuck in the cassock came right up to my armpits. It was like wearing a heavy overcoat, and the first time I led the choir up the chancel steps I tripped and fell on my face, followed by the two boys directly behind me. To add to my indignities, my mother had given me a tin of small liquorice pellets to suck (she was determined I would be best), and these shot out of my waistcoat pocket and spread over the chancel. When the procession resumed, the crunching sounded like a squad of soldiers marching up a gravel path.

I took part in all the church concerts, which were usually musical

playlets like 'Jan of Windmill Land'. I remember that for one concert we were all golliwogs and had our faces blackened by the church
helpers. As there were no facilities for washing off after the show,
I went home still covered in the boot-blacking-like substance. My
baby sister went into hysterics when she saw me and my mother
immediately applied soap and water with a scrubbing brush. Boy,
was my face red for the next few days!

Eventually I became head choir boy on the Cantori side, and faced
my arch-rival 'Blood' Owen, who was head of the Decani. We both
had hair like wire. We used to soak it in water in the vestry and then
comb and brush it and look very smart for a few minutes until it
reverted to its normal appearance of bunches of wild mint. There
was a very popular hair-cream in those days called 'Anzora', but
it was too expensive for us to buy. However, one of the boys said
it was easy to make your own: by buying a couple of ounces of gum
tragacanth, dissolving it in hot water, and adding a few drops of
mother's perfume ('Phulnana') you had the perfect hairdressing.
Well, we tried it, and the following Sunday Blood Owen and I
looked across the chancel at each other and there wasn't a hair out of
place, nor was there the following Sunday, or the Sunday after that!

We were often called upon to sing at weddings and funerals,
and at two and sixpence for a funeral against two bob for a wedding,
you can guess which of the two ceremonies we little squirts enjoyed
most. But my greatest thrill as a choir boy was when the Lady Chapel
of Liverpool Cathedral was consecrated. This was my first Command Performance. I had to sing the solo before the Archbishops of
Canterbury and York, the usual local dignitaries, and of course my
mother. 'Oh for the Wings of a Dove' and later the quartette 'God
is a Spirit' have never been sung better. I was eleven then, and a
few weeks later my mother took me to the doctor with what she
thought was a sore throat, as my voice kept cracking. The doctor
took her to one side and told her that I was growing up to be a man.
He wasn't right about the 'growing up', but the soprano voice
quickly changed into the cock-alto that you hear from me now.

At this time I was learning to play the piano and being taught
by Miss Aspinall who lived next door. This was unfortunate in one
way, as I had to practise for an hour every day and she could hear
me through the paper-thin walls. But I became very proficient at

playing scales and exercises while reading the *Magnet* or the *Gem* propped up on the music stand, and watching the clock at the same time! My mates would be assembled outside the parlour window, complete with cricket bat or football, waiting for me to finish and come out to play. We were fortunate enough to have two professional cricketers and footballers – Jack Sharp and Harry Makepeace – living in our street. They both played football for Everton and cricket for Lancashire. Of course we worshipped them, especially if they came back from training and bowled to us, a lamp-post being the wicket, or kicked the ball (actually a bundle of rags tied up with string).

The family's summer holidays were two weeks at Rhyl in North Wales. I was no trouble. My father gave me threepence a day and this was spent watching Gilbert Rogers' 'Jovial Jesters', a pierrot troupe that performed on a small wooden stage on the sands. They showed three times a day at 11 a.m., 3 p.m., and 7 p.m. (if it was wet they moved to the Town Hall), and I used to sit on the sands as close to the stage as I could get. This happened at each performance for the whole fortnight of the holidays. Father and Mother came occasionally, but they sat in the deck-chairs which cost 3d.

I usually arrived at their pitch at about 10 a.m., an hour before the show, and watched Ernie, the jack of all trades attached to the company, doing his first job of the day, whitening the shoes. These he would place at the front of the stage to dry in the sun. The performers would arrive around 10.30 a.m. and thrills of excitement would run up and down my spine. It was an all-male cast, but they had one chap who did female impersonations. His name was Cecil Barnard, but all the cast called him 'Phoebe'. I heard my mother once describe him as 'an unfortunate'. I was sitting on the sand one morning when he arrived, and I said 'Hello, Phoebe', but his retort was far from ladylike! At 11 a.m. sharp all the company in their white flannels and blue blazers would stroll on to the stage. The pianist had a cardboard box contraption in which he placed the music to prevent it blowing away. Then they would all stand up and sing the opening chorus:

> Hello – Hello – Hello!
> Jovial Jesters are we,

Full of fun and jollity
And by the rippling sea
We'll amuse you with our frivolity.
We sing – we dance,
We joke – we play
And merrily pass the time away,
For with us sorrow holds no sway
For we are the Jovial Jesters.

I knew, and still know, the words and music of every song they sang and every sketch they played. As soon as the opening chorus was over, Ernie would dash around with the collecting box to catch the people on the prom who had paused to watch. He would shout 'Last time, ladies and gents – you won't be worried again,' as he rattled the box under their noses. After about ten minutes he would dash out again repeating the same call, and so continue in this way throughout the two-hour performance. When I returned to Liverpool at the end of the holidays, I had enough material to keep all the church concerts going for the rest of the year. I think that I can honestly say the 'Jovial Jesters' gave me the bug for show business.

In 1911 we moved house again, to 58 Sandhurst Street. It was only two streets away from Rosslyn Street, but it was still a rise in the social scale, Dad having bought the house for £300. In the same year, at great financial sacrifice on my father's part, I started at the Liverpool Institute for Boys. The fees were four guineas a term, and as Dad was not earning much more than a fiver a week it was a considerable strain on the family exchequer, especially as my sister Rene had been born just four years previously.

Father was a secretary to a firm called Sugar Products. He could do shorthand, type, and add up columns of figures unlike anyone else I have ever met. When he had finished his nine-to-five chore at the office, he would come home and do the books for a number of local tradesmen, then turn to his domestic jobs like soling and mending our shoes, and he also managed to be Hon. Secretary of the local Conservative Club. Dear Dad. Later in life his job necessitated calling at a famous Liverpool brewery to supply brewing sugar, and he became somewhat inclined to sample the products.

He used to arrive home very merry, much to Mother's disgust. She always felt that she had married beneath her and could sometimes be quite snobbish when telling me whom I could play with and whom I could not. She was very Victorian and had quaint sayings like 'It is a sin to tell a lie, it is a sin to kill a fly,' or, when Dad was trimming my hair, 'Better never to be born than Sunday shorn.' She once met the wife of a local big-wig and rushed home to tell us: 'I saw Mrs Atkinson today – she moved to me'; this meant that Mrs Atkinson had nodded. My mother played the piano quite well and used to sing those funereal Victorian songs about death, and of course the hymns on Sunday – 'Here we suffer grief and pain', and 'Brief life is here our portion', etc. How I ever became a comic I'll never know!

The Liverpool Institute has turned out some famous sons over the years. I was reminded of this when I was doing a radio show in the early 1960s called 'Pop Inn'. A long-haired youth came up to me, and our conversation went something like this:

He said: 'Excuse me, sir, but I went to the same school as you did.'

I said: 'Oh yes.'

He said: 'As a matter of fact I sat at your desk, it had "A.A." carved on it, and we looked on it as a short of shrine.'

I (very flattered) said: 'Who are you?'

He said: 'Well, we're a group from Liverpool – as a matter of fact one of the other members went to the "Inny" as well.'

I said: 'What do you do?'

He said: 'Oh we play guitars and sing songs. We're well known in Germany, but we think we'll make it here eventually.'

I said: 'What do you call yourselves?'

He said: 'The Beatles.'

I (rather loftily) said: 'That's a ridiculous name, you'll never get anywhere in show business with a name like that.'

I wonder whatever became of them!

I loved my six year at the 'Inny'. I was no great scholar, but I did enjoy history and geography. Ordinary maths I could cope with, but algebra beat me, and still does. The proof of my English education is, of course, in what you are reading. I played cricket and football for the school and found that I was usually picked for the away games, either the first or second eleven. I eventually rumbled why. I was a little 'caution' and used to make them laugh on the journeys to Wallasey or St Helens, or wherever we were playing. Athletically, I have only one medal to show and that was for the 'Egg-gathering Race' for boys under fourteen. Not to be confused with the 'Egg and Spoon Race', which any idiot can compete in, the 'Egg-gathering Race' consisted of about eight eggs spaced apart over a distance of about eighty yards. The competitors had to run and grab an egg, return to base, then dash off for the next egg until they were all safely gathered in. I was very proud of myself for winning until a hated rival pointed out that because I was so near to the ground I could pick up the eggs quicker than most. I also won the singing prize, and still have my copies of Shakespeare's *Works* and *Tom Brown's Schooldays* to prove it.

There were ominous signs of the approaching Great War. The headmaster of the 'Inny' was Henry Victor Weisse, a German, who changed his name to Whitehouse. Also, there was a boy at school named Hohenrein who was a marvellous athlete and worshipped by all of us. He was obviously of German extraction; his father had a big pork shop over which the family lived. When the *Lusitania* was sunk there were riots in Liverpool, and anyone suspected of having German ancestry suffered badly. I can still see the Hohenreins' piano being flung out of the top window and the shop being set on fire.

When war broke out, I was frequently asked if I would sing to the wounded soldiers – as if they hadn't suffered enough! This I was delighted to do, not so much for patriotic motives, but because I was excused homework if the concerts were in the evening, or excused school altogether if they were in the afternoon. The tea and cakes they lavished on the artistes were an added attraction. One of my fellow performers was Tommy Handley, who was then a baritone. He would sing 'The Road to Mandalay', during which time I warbled 'Roses of Picardy', and then we combined to sing 'The Two Gendarmes', in which we thought we were both hysterically funny.

The war did not affect me that much. Life went on as usual,

revolving around school, the church, and 'The Crick'. I had also taken up dancing, and went with my three pals Billy Bird, Billy Prentice, and Norman Hockaday to Professor Dosser's Academy in Lime Street. On Saturday nights we would arrive with our dancing pumps, wrapped in brown paper, under our arms, and in anticipation of the females awaiting us inside the hall we would make full use of the scent machines which were provided at the entrance. For just 1d., we could have a squirt of 'Phulnana' or 'Shem-et-Nessin'. The girls had done the same, and the hall used to smell like a Paris brothel (whatever they smell like!). If the ladies were not up to our expectations, we would go across to the Palais de Luxe Cinema to see the lovely cinema stars of the day. Forgetting about the Waltz, the Valeta, and the Military two-step, we would be carried away in the arms of Vilma Banky, Lya de Putti, or Dorothy and Lillian Gish.

1916 came around and I had to begin looking for a job. My mother consulted the headmaster, and he asked her if I had expressed any ideas of what I would like to do. Mother said that I seemed to be very interested in the stage, but the head said he couldn't help in that direction, as the only person he knew on the stage was Sir Frank Benson and Shakespearian roles were not really suitable for me. He obviously had not thought of Bottom, the part of my anatomy I bruise every time I step off the pavement!

Most of the boys leaving school in those days went into either shipping or cotton – Liverpool's two biggest industries. (You must believe me when I tell you I was too late for the slave trade!) I sat the examinations for shipping and cotton, but without success. I tried for banks, insurance companies, and commerce, but despite all that money my father had spent on my education, I got nowhere. At last Dad came to my rescue again and managed to arrange a job for me with the Liverpool Corporation.

I was to work in the education section, in what I termed the 'Tonsils and Adenoids Department'. In other words my main occupation was sending letters out like 'Dear Mrs Cassidy, If you will present Bridget at the Fonthill Road Clinic on Friday at 11 a.m., her tonsils and adenoids will be removed.' As you will realise from the dialect, most of Liverpool's inhabitants suffer badly with their adenoids, so I was kept quite busy. I was supposed to know short-hand and typing, which I didn't. However, when the superintendent dashed into our office, glared at me and began dictating a letter, one of my pals would take down what he said while I made great play with pencil and pad. I called it the 'Askey Duployan System' – to hell with Pitmans!

My salary was around £10 a month, out of which I had to pay my dues to NALGO, and there was usually a regular collection for a wreath for some colleague who had passed away. This started me thinking: 'I will be here until I am sixty, then I'll retire on a pension and soon they will be collecting for a wreath for me!' There was my life all planned out. Would I stick it out, or make a change? Well, my mind was made up for me. Arthur Bowden Askey, at the age of eighteen, was invited to a medical with a view to joining H.M. Forces. 'I am too small,' I told myself, 'and too short-sighted. They will never accept me.' But they did!

I HAD ADDED to my repertoire while entertaining the wounded
soldiers and, in addition to 'Roses of Picardy', I was now singing
comic songs. These I had picked up at the local Music Halls which
I had started to patronise. There were dozens in Liverpool at that
time and I saw a lot of the big stars of the day: Harry Lauder,
George Robey, Wilkie Bard, and many others. I was struck by the
way they all had their own individual songs and style. One particular favourite with the soldiers was a song I pinched from a comedian
whose name I think was Morny Cash. It was about his being called
up and going for his medical and the chorus went:

> A brass band played me to the station,
> Crowds they were cheering everywhere.
> Cheer after cheer – cheer after cheer,
> My pals all bought me beer after beer.
> I must say they were very kind to me
> And a purse of gold they collected,
> But now they're going to summons me –
> They want their money back
> Just because I've been REJECTED.

And that's what I hoped would happen to me when I presented myself at St George's Hall on 6 June 1918. My best friend, Billy Bird, who was six days younger than I, came with me so that in the unlikely event of the Army accepting me, he could join up too.

Anyway, I presented the body as instructed and was told to remove my clothes. After the doctor and the orderlies had had their laugh, I was subjected to the usual indelicacies of a medical and pronounced A.1. The same went for Billy Bird, so we both went home, said our 'Farewells' and reported to Seaforth Barracks. They eventually found a uniform that nearly fitted me, together with the army issue vests and long-johns. All my life I had been what my mother termed a 'nesh'. That was the local name for someone with a sensitive skin, and I had always worn very silk-like underwear! Now I had to suffer the coarse, prickly army issues next to my lovely body, and on top of those, the rough khaki uniform with those wretched puttees which I never mastered. No matter how I wrapped them around my legs (they were miles too long anyway) they always finished up dangling over the tops of my boots. So there was Private Askey, A.B., of the Welch Regiment rigged up in his new uniform and feeling as miserable as hell. After two or three days, we were moved to Kinmel Camp in North Wales – too far away from my beloved 'Jovial Jesters' who, I heard, had females in the troupe now.

I had been at Kinmel only a few hours when my parents turned up. They were, ostensibly, on their holidays, but really wanted to be near their warrior son. I managed to scrounge a pass and walked with them from the camp to their hotel. My mother had taken my arm, and I was smoking a cigarette, when I noticed an officer approaching. As we passed, I gave him a very smart salute which he acknowledged by shouting, 'Take that cigarette out of your mouth when you salute an officer!' My mother swung round and replied with equal ferocity, 'You leave my boy alone – he didn't want to join up in the first place!'

We did not stay long at Kinmel, for we were soon posted to the Far East – Great Yarmouth. Here we lived under canvas at a place called Herringfleet. We were kept at it – drilling, fatigues, and route marches in full pack, and all the usual horrible things they think up for new recruits. Fortunately they were a grand bunch of lads, nearly all of them from the Preston and Lancaster area, and none of them Welsh. I finally stopped scratching as, gradually, I became used to my coarse army issue, and to cheer myself up started playing the piano in the canteen and singing a song when requested – or even when not requested! This paid off, as before long I was playing in the Sergeants' Mess for the weekly dance and this excused me from the early parade the following morning. I could have drunk myself silly, but in those days I was a teetotaller. In fact I had no vices, being very naïve. I even wondered why the sergeants used to disappear upstairs with their lady friends!

Eventually we moved into winter quarters at Yarmouth itself. I much preferred the billet – 13 Pier Street – to the tents we had been living in. It was a bit cold all the same, so most nights we went down to the railway where there were wagons full of coal. There we would pinch large lumps which we wrapped in newspaper, and if we passed any officers or military police we held the coal like fish and chips and pretended to be eating. On Sunday nights I did a round of the Naafi, the YMCA, the Wesleyan, and anywhere where they held concerts. They each held a competition for the best hymn-singer; first prize was a packet of twenty cigarettes. I had a very short hymn:

> He will hold me fast
> He will hold me fast
> For my Saviour loves me so-oo
> He will hold me fast.

I used to sing this, collect my prize (invariably), and then dash to the next place for yet another packet of twenty. These were always shared out back at No. 13.

Taking stock, I realised that the signallers had the cushiest job, and, in the event of eventually having to fight, they would not get too involved with the actual punch-up. This reminds me of one of my father's bathroom ballads:

> I was hiding in the ammunition van,
> 'Midst the shot and shell I'd been.
> Comrades fought – as comrades ought

> But I was nowhere to be seen.
> I was covered over with a flag
> List'ning to the sound of strife.
> When the war was o'er –
> I returned once more,
> And that's how I saved my life.

Obviously this was a Boer War ballad which Pa usually followed up with 'The Boers have got my Daddy'!

Anyway, I went in for the examination to become a signaller and to everybody's surprise (including mine) I passed. I was quite good at sending messages by flags or morse-code, but when it came to receiving the messages, I was completely lost. But once again, like my shorthand at the Education Office, I had good friends who took the messages down for me – thereby earning themselves some of my hymn-singing cigarettes.

Several army concert parties appeared at the Aquarium from time to time (I particularly remember one called 'The Red Fs' which was very good), and naturally I saw them all. I tried to start a concert party among our own fellows, but with no success. I appeared to be the only one who was stage-struck. Our main entertainment was the 'pictures', where we laughed our heads off at Charlie Chaplin. I had first seen Chaplin at the Assembly Rooms in Aigburth Road, Liverpool, which had been used as a cinema by Mr and Mrs Scott and was always known as 'Scott's Opera'. This was in the very early days of films and the chief feature was an illuminated sign under the screen which announced 'Changing Spool'. We all had to sit in the dark while Mr Scott, who hand-cranked the projector, stood in the centre aisle and fumbled to find the thread of the next reel. Our favourite occupation while this was going on was to roll a ginger-beer bottle around the floor with our feet, passing it from row to row, while Mrs Scott tried to find the culprits. Meanwhile, Mr Windus would play a selection from 'Floradora', right hand on piano and left hand on harmonium – set at right angles. Ah – Happy Days!

Life for the lads of the Welch Regiment at Great Yarmouth was fine. It was indeed a lovely war as far as we were concerned. Then on 11 November 1918 peace was declared. So great was the relief,

Billy Bird and I celebrated at the Wesleyan with a cup of cocoa! When the festivities had died down, we were warned that we would be going overseas to be part of the Army of Occupation in Germany. I had resigned myself to this when I was called to the Captain's office and told I was to be released as a 'pivotal' man. My job working for a local authority had got me discharged. Vive les Tonsils and Adenoids!

My poor pal, Billy Bird, who had joined up early to be with me, was sent off to Germany, but he was only an insurance clerk, and not a very important person like me – essential to the running of the country. Back at the Education Office I received a hero's welcome: Tonsils and Adenoids had obviously not been the same without me.

I was soon back in the old routine and had now, occasionally, started to take young ladies to the pictures. During the summer months, I would cross the Mersey to Rock Ferry to visit the Olympian Gardens. This was actually a large marquee in a field where touring concert parties appeared each week, and I saw them all: The Zeniths, The Scamps, The Brownies, The Rolling Stones, The March Hares, The Society Six, and dozens more. The proprietor of the place was a Mr Charles Boult, who later played a significant part in my life. His usual greeting to every customer was to raise his faded straw-hat, and he bid them 'Goodnight' in the same way at the end of the show. We always used to say 'Goodnight, Mr Boult! We enjoyed the show very much,' to which he invariably replied 'So pleased, so pleased.' Unfortunately he was rather deaf and one evening one of his customers said, 'I didn't think much of the show this week,' to which Mr Boult replied with his usual 'So pleased, so pleased'!

These were the halcyon days for me. I would leave the office at five and collect whomever I was taking with me (sometimes my mother) to have tea and beans on toast at Lyons, then get the boat to Rock Ferry and see the show. Then back on the ferry to catch the last No. 3 tram to the Dingle, and so to bed. I would lie awake and go through the items, noting any new jokes I had heard, and fall asleep with dreams of one day joining a concert party. I enjoyed them much more than the Music Halls, which I visited during the winter months – the whole atmosphere seemed more pleasant and relaxed.

I spent a lot of time down at 'The Crick' and became a prominent member of the tennis club, winning the silver rose bowl one year. I was a cunning tennis player: being short I developed a very sliced serve which just cleared the net, then I would rush the net to produce the famous Askey Smash. Anyone who lobbed me, of course, had me beaten. I hated mixed doubles, much preferring to play with the fellows, but as I was doing a spot of courting I had to do the necessary now and again. Our vicar, the Rev. John Eyre, had been a half-blue for tennis at Cambridge and I loved having a singles match with him, not that I ever beat him. I just had to watch my language!

About this time, a special girl came into my life. I used to see her on the train going to work each day and I couldn't keep my eyes off her. I didn't wear glasses in those days, only rimless pince-nez for reading, but I liked what I saw. Eventually I had an introduction: her name was May Swash and she was a shorthand-typist at Goodlass Walls, the paint manufacturers. We started going steady: catching the 8.30 train in the morning, the 1.05 back home for lunch, then the 1.55 back to town, and the 5.20 home in the evening. We both lived ten minutes' walk away from St Michael's station, so how we managed to get home, have lunch, then back to catch the 1.55, I shall never know. But we did. It must have been love! She had a steady boyfriend at the time and I had a steady girlfriend so things were a bit complicated; however, we resolved them without any punch-ups. Lucky for me, because he was a big fellow!

As usual, my mother vetted my girlfriends, and as this seemed to be the real thing, May came under extra scrutiny. She was not living at home owing to a difficult domestic situation, she was a year older than me – and the name Swash. This was just after the war and Mother thought it sounded German. Dad couldn't get it right and called her 'Squash' for a long time. However, my sister Rene was a great help and soon May was accepted by the family as being good enough for wonderful Arthur. May joined the church, the tennis club, and the trips to the Olympian Gardens and the theatre. Also, something important that I forgot to mention: Everton on a Saturday afternoon.

My father had four season tickets and we were avid Everton supporters, even watching the reserves rather than going to see the hated Liverpool F.C. play! It was like the clash between Rangers and Celtic in Glasgow. There would be heated arguments in my office about which team was the best. One of the clerks, Arthur Brown, punched me on the nose and broke my pince-nez when I got a big laugh out of something he said about Liverpool. But I can still remember the Everton side at that time: Fern, Downs, Mac-Donald, Brown, Brewster, Peacock, Chedzoy, Fazakerley, Dixie Dean, Crossley, and Harrison. There's a memory.

I still love football and when people ask me who I support, I always say 'Anywhere I can get in free'! I am very lucky, because I usually do! In London, the directors at West Ham and Chelsea are always pleased to see me; even my old mate Tommy Trinder will find me a seat at Fulham – that is when he is not in Hong Kong or Nairobi! In the provinces it's the same, and when I'm in Blackpool for the summer season I always go to the match on Saturday.

A few years ago my season there coincided with the Labour Party Conference. I was installed at the Imperial Hotel, where most of the prominent members of the Party were staying too. Chelsea were due to play Blackpool and the chairman of Chelsea, the late Joe Mears, had sent me two tickets for the game. I didn't need these as I was 'persona grata' at Blackpool F.C. On the afternoon of the match I was waiting at the hotel for the hall porter to call a taxi for me, when I overheard a gentleman desperately enquiring about tickets for the match. Naturally I suggested that he should make use of my spare tickets, and he thanked me with tears in his eyes – more so when I added that he need not pay for them. He called his chum 'Jim' over to join us. Fortunately I immediately recognised and knew Jim Callaghan, who then introduced me to the first gent – Lord Ted Castle (Barbara's husband). So, with my two grateful companions, I set off for the match.

At the ground I joined the Blackpool directors and observed the two Labourites enter the visiting directors' enclosure. Joe Mears, a confirmed dyed-in-the-wool Conservative, did the biggest double-take of all time when he realised that I had given them my tickets. If looks could kill then I should have dropped dead on the spot. After the game I attempted an explanation, but Joe wouldn't listen and told me never to show my face at Chelsea again. Fortunately, the next time I visited Stamford Bridge all was forgiven. Joe Mears had only temporarily turned red! Still, it taught me a lesson – beware of politicians.

I do hope you are following the plot. We have now reached the year 1921. I was planning to spend my summer holidays at Douglas in the Isle of Man and would have liked to have taken my new girl-friend May with me, but such things were not allowed in those days. I suppose this was in case the invigorating sea air put evil thoughts in our heads and we felt the urge to play Mothers and Fathers! It was a pity I could not take her all the same as this was the year I attained the age of twenty-one. I didn't want a big party or a special present, and I asked my dad for the money and he gave me twenty-one golden sovereigns. My pal Billy Bird (now back in civvies) did the same thing as he was twenty-one six days later, so we decided to have our holidays together at Douglas. We set off feeling like Paul Getty and Charles Clore (and looking much happier)! Our digs at 'Elsinore' cost less than three pounds a week, so with the money we had saved for the holiday, plus the twenty-one pounds birthday gift, the world was our oyster. We met two girls from Cleethorpes who were there on holiday and they helped us to spend our loot: half a dozen ice-creams a day hardly touched our pockets. Fun Fairs, cinemas, Music Hall (Florrie Forde at the Derby Castle singing 'Oh, Oh, Antonio'), and of course, the concert parties. And we did not want (or get) anything in return from the girls, just companionship and the feeling of 'living it up'.

There was a choice of four concert parties: Jimmy Pullen & Co. were on Douglas Head; The Nobodies were at the Palace Pavilion; Feldman's were on Onchan Head; and there was a touring concert party at the Villa Marina. Feldman's was particularly good with artistes like Elizabeth Hyde, Elsie Steadman, Alf Maynall, and a comedian called, wait for it, J. Harrington Weekes. On Friday nights they had what was called in those days a 'Go as you please' contest: this was a talent competition in which members of the audience were invited on to the stage to do their stuff. I had entered in the first week and won the first prize of two pounds quite easily.

But the day of reckoning was at hand. On the day before we returned to Liverpool, Billy and I added up the money we had left and found we were about two pounds short to settle the bill for our digs. But not to worry, I said airily – 'I'll pick up two quid at the competition

Top: In the Welch Regiment at Kinmel Camp, 1918.

Bottom: A vocal recital by Private A. Askey.

Programme

"Prologue" - - "Pagliacci" - *Leoncavallo*

"O Mistress Mine" - Shakesperian Songs *Quilter*

"Blow, blow thou
    Winter wind" -   do.   - do.

"She alone charmeth
    my sadness" - "Irene" - - - *Gounod*

Private A. Askey

"Romance" - - - - *Svendson*

"Valse Bohémienne" - - *S. Coleridge-Taylor*

Miss Evelyn K. Driffield

"Invocation to the
    Nile" - - Songs of Egypt - *Bantock*

"Honour and Arms"- "Samson" - - *Handel*

Private A. Askey

"Moonlight" - - - - *Schumann*

"The Wanderer" - - - - *Schubert*

Private A. Askey

10 minutes interval

"Air" - - - - - - *Bach*

"Madrigale" - - - - *Simonetti*

"Moto perpetuo" - - - - *Bohm*

Miss Evelyn K. Driffield

"The Toreador" - "Carmen" - - *Bizet*

"Son of Mine" - Freebooter Songs - *Wallace*

"The Gentle Maiden" - - - *Folk Song*

"The Floral Dance" - - - - *Moss*

Private A. Askey

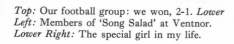

Top: Our football group: we won, 2-1. *Lower Left:* Members of 'Song Salad' at Ventnor. *Lower Right:* The special girl in my life.

Opposite: In pierrot costume for 'The Filberts'.

My first professional photograph.

tonight and all will be well.' But the Fickle Finger of Fate made itself felt for the first time in my life. Having sung Ernest Hastings' 'And yet I don't know' at the piano and received my usual applause, I stood in line with the other competitors, while J. Harrington Weekes did the 'laying on of hands'. In other words, he went along the line, putting his hand on the shoulder of each competitor in turn, and the one who received the most applause from the audience won. My applause only earned me second prize – one pound. The first prize went to two obvious professionals on holiday who played accordians. I have hated the squeeze-box ever since. Anyway, the whole thing threw the books out, and I had to wire my father for some money to get us home. And the girls had to do without their fish and chips that night. It was the end of a beautiful friendship, and also, in 1921, the end of a fortune.

Back home I started my own amateur concert party and called it 'The Filberts'. We appeared for – in fact touted for – church concerts, hospitals, old-age pensioners, children's functions, anyone who would put up with us. We wore the approved pierrot costumes of ruffles and pom-poms and sent off to Gamages in London for a communal box of grease-paints for our make-up. We applied this to our faces with great gusto: cupid's-bow lips, blue-shaded eyelids, and highly coloured cheeks. Nobody told us that it was necessary to 'powder off', and consequently by the end of a show all the paints had run one into the other and we looked like creatures from outer space! We arranged one show a year for our own benefit, usually at Crane Hall or the Balfour Institute, when we brow-beat our friends and relatives to buy tickets. By the time we had paid for the hire of the Hall, the printing, costumes, music, etc. we were lucky to break even. But what did we care – we were entertaining.

I also joined another concert party called 'The Scarletts', as the pianist. This was an essentially Catholic combination, so you can imagine how my mother felt, especially as most of our appearances were on Sunday evenings after church service. I have already mentioned the Catholic–Protestant situation in Liverpool. All the jokes in Liverpool in those days were about Pat and Mike. We never said 'Have you heard any good jokes lately?', it was always 'Do you know any Pat and Mikes?' For example, how the two football fans were returning home from a match where Liverpool, the Protestant team, had beaten Everton, the Catholic team, by six goals to nil. Pat said to Mike, 'Fancy, whack, Liverpool beating Everton by six goals,' to which Mike replied, 'Aye, there'll be some sad hearts in the Vatican tonight.'

Of course, at Christmas, I saw all the pantomimes and there were at least six at the different theatres. In one of these was perhaps the funniest comedian I ever saw – Jimmy Learmouth. His name is forgotten now, but in my opinion, and that of Tommy Handley, Jack Hylton, and I think I can say J. B. Priestley, he was the greatest. He was the Sid Field of his day, with a wonderful warm humour, but like dear Sid, he was too fond of the bottle.

At the Royal Court Theatre I began to see musical comedies for the first time and I decided that if I ever 'turned pro', that was the thing I would like to do most of all. Those I particularly liked were the touring versions of the Leslie Henson musicals. Leslie's parts were played in the provinces by Norman Griffin, and I thought 'If Leslie Henson is funnier than this chap, then he must be marvellous!' So there and then (and for a long time afterwards) I decided I wanted Leslie Henson's job. The theatrical bug had really got hold of me. I didn't like the idea of putting Leslie out of work, but after all, in show business it is every man for himself. So I wrote to the theatrical agents Grossmith and Laurilard and asked if they wanted a young, brilliant comedian. I had a letter back from the secretary of the company, a Mr Smith, saying if I was ever in London he would see me, but emphasising that I was not to make a special journey.

But that was enough for me. I had two or three days' holiday owing to me, so one bright morning I boarded the train at Lime Street bound for Euston, and my first glimpse of London. After tea at Lyons, I went to the Winter Gardens Theatre and there, from the gallery, I saw Leslie Henson. He was absolutely marvellous, but the poor fellow did not realise he was shortly to lose his job, or so I thought. The following morning I presented myself at the offices of His Majesty's Theatre, showed the letter and demanded to see Mr Smith. He was very courteous, asked me about my previous professional experiences (none!) and inferred that at the moment they were well suited with all the artistes they employed. He thanked me for calling, but told me not to bother writing to them, they would write to me if . . . The interview had taken about five minutes and I must admit I was feeling very deflated. There was nothing for me to do but get the train back to Liverpool. But I suddenly 'thought on', as they say up North. What about Daly's Theatre! I had seen musicals from Daly's played in Liverpool with a funny comedian called George Gregory playing the parts that Huntley Wright played in London. So dethroning Huntley Wright became my next objective and I hied me to Daly's in Leicester Square.

The offices were around the back in Lisle Street and on a brass plate it announced 'H. Paget – General Manager'. I asked to see Mr Paget: had I an appointment? No, but I was sure he would see me. Which he did. I told him all about myself and my ambitions and he listened very patiently. He then asked me if I would like a cup of tea. I thought, 'This is it – Daly's Theatre here I come!' But it was not to be. He talked to me very sympathetically and told me that at that moment Huntley Wright was out of work anyway as there was no part for him in the current show. As I had admitted I was in a steady job with a pension at the end of it, he advised me to go back to Liverpool and forget the theatre. After all, he said, you are twenty-two, which is really a bit late to start in the very precarious theatrical profession.

So that was it. I took the train back to Liverpool and put aside all thoughts of leaving Tonsils and Adenoids – it was to be a settled family life in Liverpool for me. I started by becoming engaged to May. We went one lunchtime to Russells in Church Street and chose a three-stone ring costing £25. As the man put the ring in the box and started to make out the bill, I whipped out my NALGO card which entitled me to ten per cent off. May was not too pleased about this; she seemed to think I was getting her on the cheap! Anyway, after two poached eggs on toast at Reece's Café (our engagement celebration) all was well. I slid back into the old routine and put all thoughts of being Leslie Henson, George Robey, Jimmy Learmouth, or even any of those lovely concert party comedians behind me.

IN THE LATE summer of 1923, May and I went over to Rock Ferry to see the last concert party of the season at the Olympian Gardens. After the show – 'The Rogues', I think it was – I said 'Goodnight' to Charlie Boult and told him how much we had enjoyed the show ('So pleased!'). I also nerved up to tell him that I was running an amateur concert party in Liverpool and he said if I gave him a list of my dates, he would try to come and see the show. That was easy, as at the time I had only one date in my diary! This was at the David Lewis Hostel some time in November. The Hostel itself was chiefly for seamen, but had quite a good theatre.

Other dates for 'The Filberts' started to come in, and I got my first real press notice in the *Liverpool Echo*. It was headed 'Ask(ey)-ing for it' and went on:

> A colleague who has seen all the local concert parties at one time or another tells me that Arthur Askey, the funny man of the 'Filberts', is far and away the best amateur comedian on Merseyside. He compares favourably with many of the pros and should he ever think of making it a whole time occupation, he feels sure he would soon be snapped up.

I felt inclined to send copies of this cutting to Messrs Smith and Paget in London, but refrained as I had now convinced myself that my future would be spent at the Education Office.

November came and we appeared at the David Lewis Hostel, and I had even forgotten that I had mentioned it to Charlie Boult. A couple of days after the concert, I received a letter from him saying he was sure I had something (though he didn't say what!) and if I contemplated going on the stage, he could put me in touch with a concert party who were looking for a new comedian, and that they would be playing at the Olympian Gardens the following May. He gave me the name of the concert party, 'Song Salad', and the address of the fellows who ran it – George Beachcroft and Martin Newman. I wrote off right away and received a reply from London saying they were willing to engage me on Mr Boult's recommendation; a thirty-week tour at a salary of six pounds ten shillings a week. At that time my salary at the Education Office was roughly three pounds a week, but, of course, I was living at home. Now I was in a real dilemma.

We had a family conference, in fact we had several. My mother, sister, and fiancée said I should chance my arm – they all thought I was brilliant (that made four of us) – but my dad told me not to be a bloody fool. Giving up a steady job, with a pension at the end of it, to go into something I knew nothing about. 'Look at what happened to Tommy Handley,' he said. 'He gave up a good job selling prams in Leece Street to go on the stage and what is he doing now? Just a chorus boy in *Maid of the Mountains*.' I consulted my boss at the office, I asked the vicar for his advice, even my pal Billy Bird, but I knew that eventually I would have to make up my own mind.

I looked around the office with its high Victorian desks, and the clerks who had been there for years just seemed to be waiting to be pensioned off. None of them had been further than New Brighton or Blackpool (except those who had served in the Army in the 1914–1918 war, which was far from being a holiday). Yet I was enjoying my life, my involvements, my friends: why take a chance? I wrote to the producers of the show and asked if I could delay my decision until after the New Year. The answer was 'No'. They must know right away, otherwise they would have to make other arrangements. That settled it. I wrote off immediately and accepted the offer. Back came my first contract: I was to rehearse at Brixton on 17 March 1924 and the show was to open at the Electric Theatre, Colchester, with a long tour to follow.

The excitement around St Michael's-in-the-Hamlet was terrific. 'Arthur Askey's going on the stage.' All the people who had told me I *ought* to go on the stage were now shaking their heads and pointing out all the risks I was taking. Except, of course, mother, sister, and fiancée. For the next few weeks I was in quite a tiz wondering if I had done the right thing, but it was too late now. I had signed the contract, for better or worse. I gave one month's notice at the office, received a farewell present in the shape of a music cabinet and a fountain pen, and left to let someone else sort out the adenoids from the tonsils.

I had heard that all theatricals had a travelling basket to carry their clothes and props in, so I bought one from the Liverpool School for the Blind. It was completely the wrong type of hamper to stand up to being humped around the country, but with 'Arthur Askey' painted on the sides it made me feel like a real pro.

I left Lime Street Station on Sunday, 16 March. Mother, sister, and fiancée came to wave goodbye and you would have thought I was going off to the Boer War! Dad did not turn up – he had washed his hands of the whole thing. But I was quite cheerful: I had half a dozen published songs and a dozen gags I had lifted from the best comedians, so felt I was well equipped for my new job.

Newman & Beachcroft, the proprietors of the concert party, had promised to meet me at Euston. I didn't know what they looked like, and they didn't know what I looked like, which was probably just as well! But when I arrived they couldn't miss me, I *looked* like an actor. With a rather loud checked overcoat, a wide-brimmed trilby, and a silver-knobbed cane, I could easily have been mistaken for Sir Gerald du Maurier – pocket size, of course. If my new guv'nors were surprised at my dress, size, and general appearance, they did not show it. We shook hands and chatted generally about hoping I would be happy and successful with them, then we collected my theatrical basket from the guard's van. This seemed to surprise them more than I did; however, we hailed a taxi, managed to get the basket strapped by the driver, and set off for Brixton where digs had been arranged for me.

We arrived at Mrs Robertson's, 9 Strathleven Road; I was told where to report for rehearsals the following morning and was left with my basket, and Mrs Robertson. She showed me my combined room on the first floor front, also where the bathroom was, then disappeared to make my evening meal. The room was very clean with a bed, wardrobe, and a wash-stand with jug and bowl. To complete the set, the third piece of crockery was underneath the bed.

Mrs Robertson appeared to know I was just beginning in show business, and was most generous with her advice. I told her I knew all the big names in Music Hall, at which she brightened and said, 'Then you will have seen the Musical Watsons.' I had to admit I had not, so she ventured, 'Well, you've heard of them, of course.' Again I had to tell the truth, so she dashed downstairs and came up with photos, bills, and press-cuttings, all proving to me that the Musical Watsons were, or had been, big time. I caved in, forgot my church upbringing and said, 'Of course I remember the act, how silly of me.' I even pretended I remembered her – the lady playing the cornet – best of all. We were now firm friends and then she said 'You know my son, of course, Wylie Watson.' I had heard of him: wasn't he the comedian who appeared with Bobby Howes and played the cello? I was now her friend for life, although I admitted I had not actually seen her son, but his fame had spread even to remote and backward parts of the country like Liverpool. Eventually she said I must be feeling tired and that she would bring my breakfast at eight in the morning as I had to be at The Volunteer, Vassall Road, for rehearsals at ten o'clock. I undressed slowly, washed and cleaned my teeth, and ignoring the third piece of crockery went along to the bathroom to 'pay the water rates'. And so to bed feeling very lonely and unsure about the whole operation. I could not phone home as Mrs Robertson had no phone and even if she had, we hadn't! A friendly voice would have helped. However, I soon fell asleep, determined that one day, I would be a big star – bigger even than the Musical Watsons.

The following morning, still dressed as an actor, I headed off for Vassall Road. There was a shop on the way announcing 'Visiting Cards printed while you wait, 100 for 2/6d'. Now I had heard that cards were an essential part of an actor's equipment. You had only to show your card at a theatre or picture house and hey presto, you were in without having to pay. So I went into the shop, and with a little help from the proprietor composed the following:

ARTHUR ASKEY

PRINCIPAL COMEDIAN

'SONG SALAD' CO.   ON TOUR

I told him I would not wait but would collect the cards after I had finished rehearsals that evening.

The rehearsals were held in the room over the saloon bar, and it was there that I was introduced to the rest of the cast by George Beachcroft, who was the light comedian, and Martin Newman, who was the baritone. George's wife, Maude Maye, was the pianist and Martin's wife, Margot Domican, was the soubrette. The soprano was Doris Lang, the comedienne Elsie la Barte, and the 'principal comedian' – Arthur Askey. The girls were busy sewing the costumes as well as rehearsing, but all day long I felt all of them had a quizzical eye on me, wondering what they had landed themselves with.

I had two programmes to cope with involving the opening chorus, sketches, duets, trios, even quartettes, but I was always a quick study and by the end of the afternoon they seemed to be quite pleased with their pot-luck comic. 'Same time tomorrow' I was told, so I went to the corner shop, collected my visiting cards and hied me to the local Music Hall: the Empress, Brixton.

I spotted the manager in the foyer, took the top card (still wet!) out of the box and presented it to him. He put in his monocle (he had a top hat as well), gave the card a quizzical look, and me an even more quizzical look. He said, 'How long have you been in the business?' I started to mutter some reply, he cut me off and said, 'Listen, son, if I was to let all the out-of-work pros in on the card, I would not have room for the few customers who are willing to pay.' So I put my card back with the other ninety-nine and went back to Mrs Robertson, to learn my words and to write letters to my mother and May, a thing I did every day of my life during my early days on tour.

The rest of the week was taken up with rehearsals and the fitting of costumes, and as the rest of the cast had done most of the songs and sketches before, and I was catching up quickly, we were given Saturday and Sunday off.

I was invited to the Beachcrofts (real name Ellis) for high tea on Sunday. We chatted about all sorts of things, professional and domestic, and by the time I got back to my digs I felt we were really getting to know each other. They were also teaching me quite a lot. They suggested I try and lose my pronounced scouse accent and not to talk about Diddy men, jam-butty factories, and treacle mines – all the gags I had been using in Liverpool. There being no radio or television in those days, this kind of patter was entirely local. Now, thanks to Ken Dodd – for my money, the funniest comedian in the business – everybody knows about it.

We rehearsed for the rest of the following week, then on the Sunday entrained for our grand opening at the Electric Theatre, Colchester. I was again lucky with my digs: Mrs Clarke at 38 Cromwell Road. Incidentally, Mother had always warned me about getting into bed with damp sheets. She was a great one for seeing things were properly 'aired'. I remember getting a pair of braces once for my birthday and when I went to put them on, there they were being 'aired' in front of the kitchen fire! Anyway the first night at Mrs Clarke's, I had the feeling that the sheets were damp. I put a mirror between the sheets, a trick my mother had said would show any dampness, but there was no 'film' on the glass. Still, I thought, better safe than sorry, so I wrapped the eiderdown around me and made myself as comfortable as possible in the armchair. Such is the influence of mothers!

So the great day dawned for my début in show business. The Electric Theatre, as its name denotes, was really a cinema. Films were shown three weeks in every four, and in the odd week touring concert parties were presented. I saw the bills around the town telling the good folks of Colchester that 'Song Salad' was appearing there nightly at 8 p.m. and, to my delight and fright, my name was in large type right across the bottom of the bill declaring that I was 'The Popular Comedian'. The first bill I saw displayed on a hoarding was close to the ground and the local dogs had already given their opinion of me!

I was at the Electric Theatre very early in the evening putting on my make-up. We all shared the same dressing room and when the two bosses arrived they made me take all the make-up off, blue eye-shadow and all, and showed me how it was possible to make-up without laying it on quite so thickly. And then they showed me how to 'powder off', for which they used Brown & Polson's Cornflour, and how to remove it at the end of the show with 'refined' lard. I was learning!

About the show itself I remember very little, except that I remembered my words. My own turn seemed to go as well as it did in Liverpool, and in the dressing room afterwards my brother and sister artistes were very complimentary. Mrs Clarke had 'been in', and when I got back to the digs she told me I was a real 'caution'! It was all she could do to stop from laughing!

We changed the programme on Thursday and again, with new songs and sketches, the show seemed to go down very well. The local paper said:

> But above all, do not fail to see Mr Arthur Askey, the 'blues' curer. The man who simply can't help making you smile – grin – and finish roaring on the way home. He is the 'King Pin' of concert party comedians.

The *Colchester Bugle* (or whatever it was called) had its record sale that day – I must have bought every spare copy! I half expected the London managers to come flocking to Colchester, but obviously the circulation of the paper was too local. Needless to say, I was feeling very pleased with my start in the business – you can imagine how my letters home were exaggerated, enclosing the newspaper cutting, of course. 'That will show my father,' I thought. Then came my first setback (after the visiting cards). The boys told me that we were out of work for the next two weeks. Our next date was at Ventnor in the Isle of Wight, the week commencing 19 April. They paid me £6 10s., my rail fare from London to the Isle of Wight, and left me to make up my own mind whether to travel back to

London with them, or return to Liverpool and face my relatives and friends. I decided I would be brave and go home, armed at least with a good press notice and the promise of about thirty weeks' unbroken tour, once I had re-started.

After a few days in purdah, I gave the silver knob on my cane an extra polish and ventured out into my old haunts, met my fiancée at her office and took her to the cinemas and theatres. I did not embarrass her by trying to get in on the card, incidentally. I called at the office, where I was told jokingly that my position was filled, and regaled my old associates with stories about life on the stage; I was just 'resting' in view of the tremendous strain of the long tour to follow. I even appeared at a church concert and upset the vicar by using the word 'hell' in one of my new-found songs. The two weeks soon passed, though not quickly enough for me. I was dying to get back and start work again. I wanted the whole country to see my talent, even those foreigners who lived on the Isle of Wight!

Like the Roman Legions a few years before me, I loved the Isle of Wight. I was to spend several happy seasons there later in my distinguished career, but more of that later. I arrived in Ventnor on a Sunday evening and went straight to the digs that had been arranged by my two impresarios. I stayed with Mrs Hooper at St Lawrence House in Albert Street and was again lucky to find a kind and understanding 'Ma'. Incidentally, the usual price for digs was between thirty and thirty-five shillings a week. That was for full board, including a hot supper after the show. If you had a private sitting room it might cost you another five bob, but at this stage I was very happy in my 'combined chat', as I had learned to call a bed-sitting room.

Monday morning I was down at the pier helping to hang the tabs (curtains) and lay out the props. The latter job was my special chore. Every Saturday night I packed the prop basket and every Monday morning I unpacked it. We had a run through the programme to refresh our memories after our triumphs in Colchester, and off we started on another week.

There appeared to be quite a good number of visitors considering it was so early in the season, and George and Martin were quite happy with the business. I had my own little dressing room in the

Pier Pavilion, very small and not helped by a fishy-smelling sack stuck in one corner. This belonged to the diver who risked his life three times a day from the Pier deck. He was quite a character. He had bought an ancient diving suit, together with the pumping machine which was worked manually by his wife. He used to make a great display getting into his gear, and before screwing on the helmet he kissed his wife in case he never returned from the perils of the deep! He would then slowly climb down the ladder into the water and his wife would start pumping madly. The rubber pipes were like sieves, and as soon as he was under water, the bubbles came up like Mother's washing day. The water at the end of Ventnor Pier was never more than five feet deep, so he had to crouch down to get totally immersed. After a couple of minutes (and in that suit he really did defy death) he came slowly up the ladder and his wife removed his helmet. He then told his audience about the fearful dangers encountered by a diver, and how thankful he was to be back on dry land again. Then came his *pièce de résistance*. He produced a small canvas bag full of sea shells, ordinary shells which can be found on any beach. 'But,' he said, 'by some caprice of nature, the Gulf Stream actually passes the end of Ventnor Pier bringing in its wake real Mother of Pearl shells of great beauty and rarity.' These he proceeded to sell to the customers at one shilling a time, and later on would go to my dressing room and fill his canvas bag from the sack in the corner, ready for the next performance. At the end of the week he gave me a bottle of Guinness and a signed photograph of himself – helmet under arm – as his cloakroom fee for leaving the sack in my room.

I began to take stock of my fellow artistes, for during the first week at Colchester I had been too engrossed with my own performance to do so. I found they were quite a talented bunch, quite worthy of supporting their principal comedian! Doris, the soprano, sang of birds and roses, while Martin belted out 'Sea Fever' and 'The Road to Mandalay'. This gave me the opportunity to crack 'Do you know "The Road to Mandalay"?' 'Yes. Do you want me to sing it?' 'No – take it!' In 1924 that gag was a riot. George Beachcroft sang Jack Buchanan songs, with dance to follow, while the soubrette – Margot – rendered dainty little numbers, also followed by a dance. Maude, the pianist, played 'Rustle of Spring' with a great flourish, and Elsie, the comedienne, had a big winner in the song about her husband who neglected her to go fishing. The final lines of the chorus:

> He's always out – tickling trout,
> Why don't he stop at home and tickle me?

got a very big laugh. I thought it was rather rude and was glad our vicar was not there to hear it.

After a pleasant week at Ventnor, we crossed the Solent on the Sunday to commence a week on the Clarence Pier, Southsea. The drawback here was the ferry boats. They used to sound their fog-horn-like sirens three times as they arrived and three times when they departed, usually during the soprano's song. They also disgorged or embarked their passengers, who tramped up and down the wooden deck of the Pier sounding like a stampede of cattle. As we had matinées every day, it got on the nerves of the cast by the end of the week. But it didn't worry me; I was acting, and wondering why I had not left the office years ago!

From Southsea, we travelled to appear in Plymouth, and the following week I made my début in London at the Crystal Palace. Again we had daily matinées, among the plants and flowers. It was like performing in an undertaker's parlour, particularly as the organist gave a recital every afternoon at the far end of the building. When he included in his repertoire such pieces as '1812' or 'Ride of the Valkyries', we did not stand much chance of being heard by the few customers in front. So my first appearance in the capital did not make any impact. I had conjured up visions of C. B. Cochran, André Charlot, or Sir Oswald Stoll dropping in, but evidently they had not read my Colchester press notice.

The next date was very important to me: the Rivoli, Liverpool. This was formerly the Assembly Rooms in Aigburth Road where I had appeared in church and school concerts and watched Chaplin films. It had been converted (slightly) to become a theatre for touring concert parties and repertory companies. Needless to say the place was booked out for the week by my relatives, friends, and a few jealous ill-wishers. We arrived at Lime Street on the Sunday afternoon and the whole company went to 'our house' for tea.

Mother had really gone to town with the tinned salmon, peaches and condensed milk, and home-made cakes, and a good meal was enjoyed by all.

I admit to being a little nervous on the Monday night; after all, most of the audience knew my jokes and songs. But they had not seen me in the concerted items and sketches and I laid into these with great gusto, overdoing everything. However, all went well and the *Liverpool Echo* was proud of me, as were the vicar and all the parishioners of St Michael's-in-the-Hamlet. Even my father admitted he had laughed once or twice, the first sign of weakening he had shown. Also, he got on famously with the rest of the company, who thought I had wonderful parents – and how right they were. They also liked my sister and, of course, my fiancée May, whom I thought was nicer than ever. We had a party one night and I persuaded May to sing. She had a lovely voice but never used it except when we had a sing-song at home, and then only after great persuasion, *and* if I played for her.

We said our sad farewells on the following Sunday and took the train to Holyhead, bound for Limerick in Ireland. I was now really seeing the world. There was a bit of shooting going on there when we arrived (even before they had seen me!) but the inhabitants did not seem to take any notice. The show went very well, though we did not break any box-office records, and the following week we appeared in Cork at the Opera House.

Our next week's engagement was at my beloved Olympian Gardens, Rock Ferry, where I had spent so many happy hours. Charlie Boult was very pleased to see me, especially as I had presented him with a case of two pipes to thank him for my introduction into the profession. My two governors had told him how pleased they were with me, so there were congratulations (and relief) all round. We had a very good week, with boatloads of Liverpudlians curious to see how I was faring and even asking for my autograph. Mother came over every night as did my sister and my May, and as we sailed back home on the ferry each night after the show I should think I was the happiest performer in the whole of show business.

After Rock Ferry, we had a week at another place that had played an important part in my life – Rhyl. 'The Jovial Jesters' were no more; there was another concert party there but it didn't attract me like the Jesters of old, even though I could now afford to sit in the deck-chairs. We appeared in the big Pavilion where, as a youngster, I used to go on Sunday nights to hear the Rhyl Municipal Orchestra and vocalists like Peter Dawson, Frank Mullings, and Norman Allin. May came over for a couple of days as, for the next few weeks, I was off to places that would keep us apart for a long time. Our next date was Cardiff for two weeks and it was there that I had my first taste of performing in the open air. We appeared at Roath Park during the first week, and Llandaff Fields for the second week, and as the weather was very kind, I quite enjoyed it. The only snag was at Llandaff where there appeared to be a plague of greenfly, and I must have swallowed hundreds during the week. From Cardiff we went to Penarth to appear in the Pier Pavilion. Business there was very poor, but the manager always had an excuse for the lack of customers: Monday they don't come in until they hear what the show is like; Tuesday it rained and they will not walk the length of the Pier in the wet. Wednesday there was a whist drive in the Town Hall, and Thursday it was blowing a gale. Friday, well that was always the worst night as people had no money, and Saturday, there was a thunderstorm and hail-stones. After the show on Saturday night when the manager and Martin were reckoning up the percentages, I heard the manager say, 'Sorry, Mr Newman, the business has not been too good on account of everything,' and Martin replying, 'I think the only chance of doing a good week here would be in a dense fog!'

From Wales we travelled to Glasgow where we played for two weeks on bandstands in the parks. It was the first time I had been north of the border and I really felt I was getting around. Our last appearance in Glasgow was at Kelvin Grove – the Palladium of the parks – with proper dressing rooms and a real stage, though still al fresco. We appeared on stage at seven o'clock precisely and belted into our opening chorus. There was no reaction or applause when we finished, so we started our second concerted item. About half-way through, an attendant wandered up to the front of the stage and pointed out the show at Kelvin Grove 'didna starrrt' until 7.30 p.m. We could not see if there was anyone out front as the sun was very low and blinding. Anyway we went back to our dressing rooms and began the show again at 7.30 p.m., fortunately to a packed and appreciative audience.

On Sunday morning we entrained for Hereford where we were to appear at the Garrick Theatre. This was run by a Mr Reginald A. Maddox, on whom I evidently made an impression because he asked me if I would see him in his office one morning and offered me pantomime at twelve pounds a week. Was I excited – the offer was nearly double what I was getting with 'Song Salad'. The panto was to be *Little Miss Muffet* opening at South Parade Pier, South-sea, for three weeks, then a six-week tour to follow. And I was to play Dame. I signed with alacrity (better than a pen), and was congratulated by the rest of the company, none of whom had arranged pantomime dates at the time.

Our next two weeks were at Ilfracombe and Bedford where May joined me to spend her holidays, and she was as excited as I was about my pantomime engagement. We felt my career was really going in the right direction. We said our fond farewells on the Sunday, she returning to Liverpool while I travelled to Weymouth for our next week's engagement. This was the week of 11 August and it was there, at the Alexandra Gardens, that I did my first broadcast. A box-like contraption was put up in front of the stage and we did part of our normal show for about half an hour. I was not over-impressed by it all, not realising what an important part radio was to take in my future career.

From Weymouth to Worthing, then on to Brighton where we appeared twice daily at the Aquarium. At the matinées, there were far more fish than patrons, but at least the fish in their tanks gave us something to play to. A regular patron at the matinées was an ec-centric millionaire named Cunliffe. He used to have a whistle strapped to his wrist and carried a small hatchet in his pocket as he was terrified of being trapped in a fire. But what a character he was! He would take the seven of us into all kinds of shops and buy us anything from lobsters to wrist-watches. He was of Scottish extraction, and when our tour had finished we went to his home in Hove and had a week of 'Afternoon at Homes', each of us doing our own thing. In front of each chair was a table with a lighted candle so nobody would disturb the entertainment by daring to strike a match to light a cigarette. He would oblige with a Scottish

Above: May's debut with 'Song Salad'.

Right: The first Dame, in pantomime at Southsea—influenced by Dan Leno.

FRED WILDON'S ENTERTAINERS

Upper Left and Middle: On stage at Shanklin. *Lower Middle:* With Charlie Harrison in 'Babes in the Wood', Nottingham, 1933. *Upper Right:* About to sing 'The Bee'. *Bottom:* King of the Masonics

Opposite Top and Middle: Fred Wildon's Margate Entertainers. *Bottom:* Powis Pinder's 'Sunshine Company' at Shanklin.

Top: 23 March 1925: May and Arthur Askey, with family and friends. *Middle Left:* With mother and May at Margate, 1929. *Bottom:* Left holding the baby! *Middle Right:* May, Mother, Anthea, Dad and me, on the beach at Shanklin.

song or two which really was the whole object of the exercise. He was stage-struck.

After Brighton, we went to Taunton, Torquay, Exmouth, Morecambe, and finished the tour at Dalton-in-Furness and Millom in Cumberland. I remember the latter date as the theatre, a miners' institute, had gas footlights. And as Christmas was getting near, we did a special children's matinée, advertised as a 'potted pantomime'. We actually did part of our normal show, but called each other 'Buttons' or 'Prince Charming' and then got the kids up on the stage to sing, dance, or recite to kill the rest of the afternoon. But I expect we took about a fiver at the doors and it all helped.

So my first season with 'Song Salad' had ended. They offered me a contract for the following year, but I told them I was hoping to get married in the spring and was looking for a resident concert party, because if I was to tour, I would have to pay my wife's fare. They came up with a great idea. They would book May, my future wife, as the soprano, having seen her and heard her sing at the party at 'our house'. And they would pay us a joint ten pounds a week. May had never appeared in public in her life, but she agreed to take singing lessons (so keen was she to marry me!) and so the deal was on. We even decided that she would make her professional début as May Bowden, which you may remember was my mother's surname and my middle name. I signed the contract, then headed back to Liverpool to spend a couple of weeks at home, catch up with a bit of courting, and get ready for my first pantomime.

I had to supply my own wardrobe for the part of Dame, so my mother, sister, and May were kept very busy making or altering some of their own dresses while I looked around the second-hand shops for a feather boa, spring-sided boots, and the usual Dame accessories. I bought a red wig with a centre parting and a bun at the back just like the one I had seen George Robey wear, and two weeks before Christmas I said my farewells once again and took the train to Portsmouth. I felt completely confident. I was at last climbing in the dicey world of show business.

NOTHING LIKE A DAME

I HAD SEEN a pantomime in rehearsal in Liverpool while I was 'clerking' at the Education Office. At that time, every pantomime had a troupe of children called 'Sunbeams', 'Dainty Dots', 'Manchester Mites', even 'Breezy Babes'. As they were under age, they had to have a licence to perform and comply with regulations such as being out of the theatre by nine o'clock at night. It was the duty of the School Attendance Department to see that the latter rule was carried out. So I went up to the Olympia Theatre to see the dress rehearsal of Julian Wylie's *Dick Whittington* – starring Ella Retford and that very funny comedian Harry Weldon. I had no right there at all, but I told the stage-door keeper I was from the Liverpool Corporation Education Offices and was soon ushered in (with a certain coolness) by the manager. I was, of course, fascinated. Sitting in the stalls of this huge theatre with Julian Wylie – then one of the most important producers – and about half a dozen of his staff just a few seats away.

It was pretty cold, the usual thing when rehearsing pantomimes. The heating system in any theatre is for the prospective customers, not the artistes. Ella Retford rehearsed with a fur coat over her tunic and tights, and Harry Weldon was keeping warm with something out of a bottle, which became more obvious as the evening wore on. But I didn't feel the cold at all. It was all magic to me and even 'going back' time after time made it all the more pleasurable.

As the children's deadline grew nearer, I could see worried faces looking in my direction as they had only rehearsed the first half of the pantomime. Eventually one of Julian Wylie's minions came and asked me if it would be possible for the children to stay on a little longer as they had an important scene in the second half. I gave the matter some thought and then airily said it would be all right, if it was not too late! I received grateful nods from Wylie and company and personal thanks about midnight, with the kids still there! The only one who had no right to be there was me!

Rehearsals for my pantomime at Southsea were very similar, though on a smaller scale, of course. The principal comedian was Will Seymour, a charming man and the son of a vicar. In the summer he ran his own concert party called 'Bubbles' and at one time Richard ('Stinker') Murdoch and Kenway & Young were in the cast. He helped me considerably and we remained friends for many years afterwards. The other comic was Bert Elmore, a rougher type steeped in the Music Hall tradition, but again a very nice fellow. We all three shared the same dressing room, and poor Bert, who suffered from asthma, was continually burning herbs and inhaling the fumes. It helped the congestion in his lungs, but not the congestion in the dressing room! Opening night came and on my first entrance I had to take a kick at Bert, who was 'Simple Simon'. I was wearing a tight hobble skirt and as I kicked out at him it pulled my other leg from under me and I fell flat on my back. It got a very big (and, for me, unexpected) laugh, but it was about the only one that night. I was partly saved by the item before the palace scene at the end. This was a duet called 'Brighter Clergy' with Will Seymour as a vicar and me – hitherto a female throughout the show – as a curate! I have learned through the years that you can take all sorts of liberties in pantomime, but this was ridiculous. But I felt happier doing it than I did playing Dame.

With the help of Bill Seymour and Bert Elmore, I think I improved with each performance, but I still did not feel right in skirts. We ran for about four weeks at Southsea, then went on tour to theatres like the Theatre Royal, Guildford, the Theatre Royal, Taunton, etc., all of which have now disappeared. Probably I started the rot! Dear old Robb Wilton once said, 'I'm playing the Chelsea Palace this week – it closes down on Saturday and if that's a success, they're closing down all the others.'

The boss of our panto, Reg Maddox, had an option on my services for the following year's pantomime at an increased salary of fourteen pounds a week but he did not take it up, which verified what I had already realised – I was 'nothing like a Dame'!

I went home to start making arrangements for my forthcoming marriage.

May had come down to Southsea to see me in the panto and my performance had not put her off or weakened her love and faith in me. So on 23 March 1925, Arthur Bowden Askey and Elizabeth May Swash, both of this Parish, were joined together in Holy Wedlock by the Rev. John Eyre. St Michael's-in-the-Hamlet Church was crowded – you can always draw a full house when it's free – and I had the choir to help things along. When it came to settling up I found that the fees had gone up since my day and it was now two and six for a wedding, the same as a funeral.

Our honeymoon was one week at the Imperial Hotel off Russell Square in London. Every evening was spent at one theatre or another. One show I particularly remember was *The Street Singer* at the Lyric, with Phyllis Dare and a popular comedian called A. W. Bascombe. During the show, May said she felt sick (What – already!) and had to go out. I was too engrossed with what was happening on stage and made no effort to leave with her. However, a woman sitting the other side of her obliged, even to the point of getting May a brandy. May came back in the interval looking ghastly, and the woman gave me a right rollicking for being so inhuman. May did not feel too happy about my behaviour either and we had our first little tiff. The whole episode gave great credence to a song Bascombe had just sung in the show, 'Gawd – how I hate women' with the tag line 'I hate 'em like hell'!

After our week of living it up, we left the Imperial on the Sunday to travel to Brixton where we were to prepare for my second, and May's first, season in concert party. We stayed with Mrs Robertson, my first landlady. She was most kind and obviously took to my new bride, as did everyone else.

As I was now married, we planned to start catering for ourselves and just pay the landladies for the rooms and the cooking of meals. It meant we could eat what we wanted instead of some of the hideous concoctions which were sometimes served up. I had found that some landladies preferred you to buy your own food, but when I was single and on my own, I used to cajole them to do the catering for me. I well remember being very bewildered in my early touring days when one landlady asked me if I would like her to 'caper' for me!

At rehearsals everybody helped May. She soon learned her bits and pieces in the show, and as she was a complete amateur I felt very proud of her. We started the tour at Ventnor, where it became obvious that May's nervousness was something we would have to cope with. She was fine in all the concerted numbers and sketches, but during her solo turn her nerves got the better of her. However, we found a solution. She only felt confident if I accompanied her on the piano, but I had to be very careful because the audiences were always looking in my direction to see if I was going to do something funny. But I put on my pince-nez and kept a very straight face, and May was received very well.

Our tour comprised several of the same dates as the previous year, with the addition of Folkestone where they had tea matinées every day and the show went on to the accompaniment of rattling cups and saucers. We also played Ashford in Kent, Burnham-on-Sea, Bognor, Cromer, Emsworth, Norwich (where May got a marvellous notice in the local paper), and the Manchester parks, like Glasgow, on bandstands in the open air. We played Glasgow parks again, followed by a week at Dunoon.

And so we finished my second tour with 'Song Salad'. They offered us the next season which I accepted with the proviso that if I had the offer of a resident season they would release me. This they agreed to, which was just as well for me as things turned out. Meantime, I was getting worried about pantomime. I had received no offers and had auditioned only for the Grand Theatre, Brighton, where I was told they 'would let me know', which I realised meant that I had not got the job. Incidentally, this was the only audition

I ever did in my theatrical life. Not like the girl who went around for years doing auditions with no success at all. However, one day she did her usual routine and prepared to pack up and go when the manager called her back and told her she had got the job. She looked at him in amazement and said, 'I'm sorry, I only do auditions.'!!

Out of the blue, I was offered a part in the pantomime at the Theatre Royal, Torquay, with a tour to follow. The salary was eight pounds a week, which was to include May in the chorus. After my previous pantomime salary of twelve pounds this was a real comedown, but work was work and I accepted. After all, we could live comfortably on four pounds a week, we liked Torquay, and, being newly married, we would have been happy on five pounds a week in Barnsley. So after two or three weeks in Liverpool with our folks, we set out for glorious Devon to appear in Carlton Frederick's *Babes in the Wood*.

I found I was to play a nondescript part and had to understudy the principal comedian while May understudied the principal girl. If either of them had been off, we would have got a few extra bob, but unfortunately they were healthy creatures and did not miss one performance. I dressed with the two Robbers, a couple of real old-timers who used to exit after the fight scene, show me their bruises and say, 'That one got a big laugh,' or, with a larger scar, 'That one got a yell.' They were exhausted after their fight and used to crawl off the stage and sit with their backs to the wall, panting and puffing. When they had partially recovered their breath, one would always turn to the other and groan 'Success after success'! It was a very happy pantomime and Mrs Pike, our landlady, was a real dear. I had a very good notice in the local paper:

> Arthur Askey as 'Buttons' is immensely amusing. One would like to see him afforded even greater chances for attacking the risible faculties because there seemed to be a reserve of power and talent behind everything he did, which was not called into full play.

I knew this of course, but it was nice to see it in print!! We had about eight weeks in Torquay, the weather was lovely, and I remember a press picture being taken of us all rehearsing on the sands.

The tour following Torquay at the beginning of 1926 started at Taunton and eventually finished with three nights at Weston-super-Mare, three nights at Tiverton, and a week at Stroud. At the latter place we had trouble finding digs and eventually settled in a house with 'Beam's Breezy Babes', who were the juveniles in the panto. There were sixteen of them, looked after by Mrs Beam and a matron. What a noisy houseful it was, and the big snag was that there was only one combined toilet and bathroom which meant a long and frustrating queue in the mornings.

From Stroud, May and I returned home to Liverpool. This I was determined to do if only to show off my latest press notice to all and sundry. I could have saved myself the trouble, as I had sent a copy to my mother who had proudly shown it to the whole of Lancashire and Cheshire. After about three weeks we set off for London again to rehearse for our third tour with 'Song Salad'. I had been tipped off that Fred Wildon, who ran the Margate Entertainers, was coming to see me work as he was looking for a new comedian. I told Newman and Beachcroft about this so that they would be prepared if I impressed Fred Wildon. Sure enough, he came to see me at Ventnor (where we opened) and offered me a summer season at Margate at twelve pounds a week.

Although May had done very well in 'Song Salad', I knew it was an ordeal for her every time she had to do her turn, and so I accepted the Margate offer on my own. Martin and George were very sorry to lose me and, for my part, I was very grateful for their help. They had lined up a comedian called Al Maurice to take my place. I had never met him, but he used to put funny adverts in the theatrical papers from time to time. I remember one he had in *The Stage* which read: 'Al Maurice will exchange wife's fur coat for routine of patter new to South Wales.' On another occasion he took the front page of *The Performer* and had it laid out like a diary. It started 'January 1st, Vacant. January 8th, Vacant. January 15th, Vacant', and so on until 'July 18th and 25th – Holidays', and then the rest of the year: 'Vacant – Vacant – Vacant'.

So May and I packed our bags, said our farewells and travelled back to London. First of all we stayed at digs I had seen advertised in *The Stage*. They were in Angel Road, Brixton, and we had a basement room. The first night we woke up to discover the bed and walls infested with bugs. Naturally we couldn't sleep and the following morning I went to the Post Office and sent myself a telegram reading 'Come home at once – father ill.' When it was delivered I announced the news, telegram in hand, to the landlady. She demanded a full week's rent, but at least we could leave the place without causing a scene. Which proves what a lily-livered coward I am. We then stayed with Mrs Collar in Edwardes Street, New Cross, who was a friend of Mrs Beam of 'Breezy Babes' fame. We were offered a very pleasant combined room, with piano, and Mrs Collar proved a real gem. Here the only snag was that the bath was in the kitchen, covered by a board which served as a table. But on Saturday nights the board was removed and everybody – Mr and Mrs Collar and their daughter, May and I – had a bath. Not at the same time, I hasten to add. We were gradually learning to live with these inconveniences!

This was 1926 and the General Strike had just started. I had to get from New Cross to the West End for rehearsals, but managed somehow to get there on time. I walked a lot and travelled on lorries or the few buses that were running (with the drivers protected by wire netting), and got an occasional lift from a motorist. We rehearsed in a church hall in West Street and when the pianist struck the first chord on the piano, half a dozen mice ran out. My new governor, Fred Wildon, was a great character. He was an all-round entertainer who sang songs, cracked jokes, played the one-string fiddle, and could also do conjuring tricks. The rest of the company were Lilian Myers, soprano, Lucas Bassett, tenor, Doris Lee, comedienne, Geoffrey Dupree, entertainer and dancer, Stoll and Steward, a husband and wife comedy act, baritone Horace Rose, and pianist Cyril Weller. I travelled to Margate on the Saturday with Stoll & Steward in their bull-nosed Morris, and arranged digs for the whole summer in Clifton Gardens, Cliftonville.

Fred Wildon's Entertainers were employed by the Margate Corporation, as were Murray Ashford's Entertainers – who were considered as the friendly opposition. We alternated at two venues, the Oval and Westbrook Pavilion. We also did matinées at the Oval on alternate days, and if wet, in the Winter Gardens. The Oval was a bandstand surrounded by 2,000 seats: ninepence for the deck-chairs and sixpence for the wooden seats. The dressing room was under the floor of the bandstand and was reached through a trap-door in the stage, then down about twelve wooden stairs. Here we kept all our props and also a bucket as a toilet facility. I don't remember it ever being used, which was just as well as there was nothing to separate the boys from the girls.

Promptly at 3 p.m. and again at 7 p.m. we would all climb the stairs with our necessary props, usually just hats of all kinds, and start the opening chorus. Woe betide anyone who had forgotten their props, because this necessitated raising the trap-door during somebody's turn, disappearing, and re-emerging with the forgotten article. There were, of course, no microphones in those days, so one had to belt out to be heard over the sound of the sea, the children, dogs barking, cars hooting, and even the occasional plane on a pleasure flight. That is where I learned to 'project' my voice – a lost art these days. There is a story about an old Music Hall performer who could not be heard in the gallery and they started to give her the 'bird'. They whistled and hooted and threw pennies until a chap rose in the stalls, looked up at the gallery and shouted, 'Give the old cow a chance,' to which she replied, 'Thank God there's one gentleman in the audience!'

I used to arrive just before the show started, dressed in my lounge suit for the matinées or dinner jacket in the evenings, and as I became more popular with the Margate audiences, I received rounds of applause all the way down the terraced steps until I disappeared through the trap-door. It did my ego good. Of course we were rained off now and again, which I hated, although it did not affect my salary. If it rained in the afternoon we appeared at the Winter Gardens or, if it was not our turn, we would go and watch the opposition to see who had the better show.

The Winter Gardens usually had variety bills, ballet companies, or that type of entertainment once nightly. One week, the famous Co-Optimists came to play there. It was actually the swan-song for this fabulous show, a star-studded concert party that had played in the West End for years. The cast were Davy Burnaby, Gilbert Childs, Laddie Cliff, Melville Gideon, Betty Chester, Elsa Mac-Farlane, Wolesley Charles and Stanley Holloway. One afternoon as we emerged from the 'salt mines', as I had christened our dressing room, the whole cast of the Co-Optimists were sitting out front in deck-chairs. We were all very excited and hurriedly switched to our best songs. We had five programmes, so naturally some of the numbers were weaker than others. After the show, we disappeared down the trap-door and when I came up, Stanley Holloway was waiting for me. He said, 'You're a funny little fellow – you're going to be a big star one day.' He was the first big 'name' I had ever met and needless to say, I was very thrilled.

The method of collecting the money at the Oval is worth mentioning. Not a penny was taken until the first notes of our opening chorus, then the collectors got busy with their ticket-punches. So during the first two or three items, usually concerted numbers, we were accompanied by the piano and the tinkling of the bell-punches. The head collector, Kimpton, could time the weather to a nicety and would often pop his head down the trap-door and say 'You'd better get started – it'll rain in ten minutes,' so we'd commence five minutes earlier than advertised to get the loot in before the bad weather. Even then we would have some stalwarts who would sit it out with raincoats and umbrellas until Fred went forward and gave an impassioned speech about it 'not being fair to them and not being fair to us – we had our voices to think about,' etc. So the hardy ones would pack up and go. As I used to say about the people in the sixpenny seats which were iron-framed, wood-slatted fold-up chairs: 'Whatever you think of the show, you will all go away with the same impression!'

During this summer of 1926 a well-known provincial pantomime producer – Fred Clements – saw the show and offered me a contract for three pantomimes at a salary of twelve pounds rising to fifteen pounds. Clements had his own concert party at Arcadia, Skegness, which he made his headquarters. He died about the same time as C. B. Cochran who left nothing, whereas Fred Clements – small fry in theatrical circles – left about £150,000. My first panto with him was to be *Jack and the Beanstalk* at the Theatre Royal, Sheffield. He also gave my May a contract for the chorus at two pounds ten shillings a week. So things were coming up roses, and it would be an understatement to say I was very happy.

WHEN THE show finished at Margate, I went back to London and stayed with Cyril Weller, the pianist, at his house in Bromley, Kent. I was then introduced to a branch of the business I did not know existed. It was to become my main source of income for the next twelve years – after-dinner entertaining: Masonic lodges, City companies, staff dinners, as well as Central Hall concerts, National Sunday League shows, etc. I started quietly with perhaps two or three appearances a week and gradually worked up to doing an average of four a night. The usual fee was two guineas, often less ten per cent for the agent, and for that I had to do two appearances. Later on when I became 'King of the Masonics', I would only do one appearance and upped my fee to three guineas, or even five for a Ladies' Night.

At this time, however, I was glad to get the odd booking, and some of them were very odd. I have a programme for a Post Office staff concert where the artistes were all employees with the exception of myself. It read something like 'Miss May Smith – soprano, Mr George Robinson – bass, Mr Fred Jones – violin,' etc., and then at the bottom it just said 'A. Askey – professional'! Made me feel like a leper.

Every Saturday night in the autumn I was at the North End Hall, Croydon, with Fred Wildon's Margate Entertainers, and on Sundays at one of the National Sunday League Concerts. These were held at all the London and suburban Music Halls, from the Palladium down to the South London Palace. Eventually I was to do two or even three of these on a Sunday night. They were very 'polite' concerts, and I had to be an entertainer rather than a comedian. No props like funny hats were allowed, and double acts like Elsie and Doris Waters or the Western Brothers were booked provided they did not talk to each other – they just had to sing.

Another booking where one had to be careful was at the Wesleyan Central Halls. I have often done four of these on a Saturday night, starting, say, at Barking, then on to East Ham, Hackney, and Islington. The parson usually sat on the platform while you worked and at Islington the gentleman in question was Dr (now Lord) Donald Soper. After I cracked a gag, he would spring up and say 'What Arthur says is so very true – a woman should always be in the position to ask her husband where he has been', and would rabbit on while I was glancing at my watch, hoping I would not be late for my next appearance, with such a tight schedule.

My bookings in London were coming in so nicely, I began to feel sorry I had contracted for pantomime. However, two weeks before Christmas, May and I packed our bags and set out for Sheffield to stay with Mrs Aves at 720 Abbeydale Road. Rehearsals were very pleasant and the people were nearly all concert party types, whom I always found much 'softer' than Music Hall artistes. I was again third comedian and understudy to the principal comic, Rob Currie, who played Dame Durden. His throat began to sound wonky at rehearsals and after the two shows on Boxing Day, he was voiceless. I arrived at the theatre the following day for the matinée and found the wardrobe mistress putting large tucks in all the Dame's clothes. I was 'on'. No rehearsal or anything. But I had watched Rob carefully and knew every word and every move. So, nothing daunted, on I went and was a big success. Fred Clements rushed around after the show and said he would pay me two pounds a performance every time I went on, and as Rob was off for two weeks I did rather well. I'm sure the guv'nor could have bitten his tongue off as he didn't leave £150,000 for nothing. I got all the laughs that Rob had got and my only failure was in the serious bit where Jack, the principal boy, came back from the fair and told me he had sold Daisy, the cow, for a bag of beans. Rob Currie used to do a great piece of drama with this bit. The audience was deathly quiet as he took the bag of beans and said, 'What – a bag of beans for Daisy – our cow – our ALL? What have you done, boy – what have you done?' at the same time throwing the offending bag of beans through the window. It was one of the great moments of tragedy in the annals of the theatre. Unfortunately, I got roars of laughter when doing it. The principal boy had me in her dressing room (I mean that in the nicest way) and went through the scene with me over and over again, but I could not get it right – so we agreed that I should play it for laughs. They say that every comedian wants to play Hamlet, but if I had had any ideas in that direction this experience convinced me it would have been a waste of time.

May enjoyed her chore in the chorus and let me into a little secret about the girls. I used to notice that in the palace scene, where the girls always had to walk down a set of stairs, on a Saturday night they always seemed to totter. May revealed that the girls were not tipsy, but had their wages in their shoes: there were no pockets in their clothes and they dared not leave the money in the dressing rooms. So they would wobble on with two golden sovereigns and four half-crowns pressing into the soles of their feet.

Of course my mother, father, and sister came to see the genius at work in the pantomime and Pa ventured to remark that he thought I was 'getting on nicely'. We had about ten weeks at Sheffield, then returned to London where I picked up a few more after-dinner concerts and re-joined Fred Wildon on Saturdays at Croydon.

The summer season came around again, so off we went to Margate. There were two or three changes in the cast and, for my part, there was a happier atmosphere than the previous season. But the weather was very bad. We were 'rained off' time and again throughout June and July. Fred was on a percentage with the Corporation and even he, usually indestructible, started to get depressed. However, August came in with a spell of glorious weather and we had two thousand people at every performance at the Oval. Fred was leaving more of the comedy to me, so at matinées, after the opening chorus, he would settle in his chair, doze off, and only wake up in time to do a turn with his one-string fiddle. He liked a gin or two at lunch and that helped him to drop off. One hot afternoon, Lilian Myers, our soprano, sang her song and announced her encore. She said, 'Ladies and Gentlemen – "April is a Lady" ' and Fred, fast asleep, said quite audibly, 'July was a bit of a bugger.' The audience heard it and the laugh woke Fred from his snooze!

He was quite a good golfer and he introduced me to the game that I love so much. Through the years, I never improved on a 16 handicap, but I never worried about my game. I just enjoyed walking around in the fresh air and hitting the occasional good shot. I eventually became President and Captain of the Stage Golfing Society. We had an annual dinner at the Savoy and provided our own entertainment. One year I was asked to do a short golfing duet with our previous president, Laurence Olivier. It was only about twelve lines of a song with three or four lines of dialogue, so we arranged to meet at the Stage Golfing Club over the Salisbury Arms in St Martin's Lane to run through the number. The dinner was on the Sunday, so we met on the previous Monday and went through it – and through it – and through it. Larry then had to get off to the theatre, so I said, "I'll meet you at the Savoy on Sunday about 6.30 (the dinner was at 7.30) and we'll go through it again.' He said, 'Sunday! Tomorrow!!' So every day we rehearsed and this certainly taught me a lesson in how to become a perfectionist.

At the end of the season (1927) I returned to London and again stayed with the Wellers at Bromley. My concert dates were on the increase and I was getting to be 'known'. Not that everybody got my name right. I was called Ashby, Ashcroft, Lasky, Tasker, or 'Are you the little fellow with the glasses?'! I remember someone telling me that Askey was not a good name commercially and suggesting I used my second name Bowden. I am naturally glad I did not take their advice. The A.A. initials stood me in good stead in later years because whenever I was asked to appear at an All Star show, I used to insist on the billing being done in alphabetical order. In consequence I have been on bills with Maurice Chevalier, Gigli, Gracie Fields, etc., and I have always been top.

Of course, when artistes give their services, there should be no star-billing. I used to be booked at Sunday concerts where all the other artistes were big names and giving their services. In these early days, I was paid three guineas to stand by all evening in case there was an occasion when any of the big names were not there, as they dashed between theatres. I would be pushed on and just get going, when a star would arrive and I was asked to 'kindly leave the stage' until the next emergency occurred. Still it was worth it, for apart from the three guineas, I was able to rub shoulders with some of the big names of the day.

Soon it came time to rehearse for my second pantomime with Fred Clements. The subject was *Sinbad the Sailor* at Plymouth and again I was third comedian and understudy. There were none of the previous panto's artistes amongst the cast, but they were a nice friendly crowd, all chiefly from concert party. The principal comedian was Fred Beck, who ran his own concert party in the summer with his wife Dorrie Dene, a very good comedienne.

Back to London and more concerts, then down to Margate again for my third season. I was by this time an established favourite with the visitors – and the residents – and the local papers used to eulogise about me quite a bit. The *Daily Mail* ran a competition with headlines like 'Who is your favourite? Seaside Artists' chance of fame.' Readers were invited to act as searchers for new talent. The *Mail* had run a similar stunt in 1920 and produced Gillie Potter and Randolph Sutton. Anyway, the competition went on all through the summer and posters began to appear saying 'Margate Comedian heads poll'. I hardly dared hope it was me since there were two much better-known comedians performing in Margate. Leonard Henry was at the Pavilion on the Jetty, and he was becoming very well known on the radio, vying with Tommy Handley in popularity. I met Leonard on the promenade one morning and he said, 'I see the *Daily Mail* has discovered me – a bit late, aren't they.' Also, at the Lido, was Leslie Fuller, who had appeared in some early British talking films and was certainly quite famous. I met Leslie and he said almost the same as Leonard: 'Fancy running a competition to discover me!' When the result was published, guess who was top of the poll for the whole country? Me! I remember going back to the digs, where the landlady had displayed dozens of posters saying 'Margate Comedian Wins'. They were hanging all over the house, inside and out.

I thought this was to be my big break and sat back and waited for the offers to pour in. However, the *Daily Mail* critic who came down to see me was not as enthusiastic as the readers had been. His notice read:

SEASIDE SEARCH TALENT
MR ARTHUR ASKEY
COMEDIAN

YOUNG MAN WITH POSSIBILITIES

Margate, Saturday

Mr Arthur Askey is a very short man with red hair and a pair of very large horn-rimmed spectacles.

He is a member of the concert party which Mr. Fred Wildon runs at the Oval here.

For the last fortnight postcards have poured in from readers of The Daily Mail resident or holiday-making at certain specified South of England seaside towns recommending the merits of this and that concert party comedian or comedienne. Mr. Askey's name has been on a great many of them.

Well, to-day I have watched Mr. Askey. He showed symptoms of being able to amuse in a way of his own. Physically he reminded me of Mr. Nelson Keys; in methods he is not so glitteringly definite and clear-cut. He is slower and his face is not so elastic.

I thought his material was poor, but that he handled it with assurance and with a voice that carries well. He did not dance, but he looks as if he could.

At present I should not put Mr. Askey down as being ready to step into a leading part on the West End stage, but he is a young man with possibilities.

I found later that the critic who wrote the review, William Pollock, had attended a Saturday afternoon matinée, when we always held Children's Talent Competitions ('No recitations'), and hence the tepid notice. We hardly did any work, but left it to the kids.

Top: The Austin 16 and family, 1936. Middle: The Hudson at Hammersmith, 1939. Bottom: The Mercedes, more recently.

Top: The 'Band Waggon' gang. *Left:* With Lewis the goat. *Above:* Pioneer days on radio, teaching Julie Andrews a thing or two.

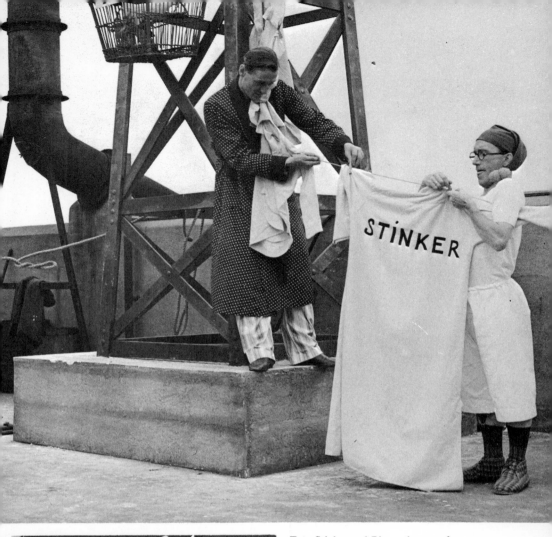

Top: Stinker and Big at the top of Broadcasting House.

Left: The First and only edition of Arthur Askey's Annual, 1939

My weekly spot in 'Radio Fun'.

The season finished, and May and I returned to London to our new flat – our first home – at 24B Golders Way, over a shop in Golders Green Road. The furniture was on the 'never-never', but after paying one instalment I felt it was a stigma and went and settled for the full amount. Mother sent 'my piano' from Liverpool; how the men got it up the stairs and into the flat I shall never know. There were about thirty outside steps up to the first flat – 24A – then another twenty or so up a narrow staircase with a bend in it to reach ours. We had a coal fire in the lounge, and the coal bin was in the yard down all the stairs. The first time I brought up a scuttle of coal I tripped as I entered the flat and shot the coal all over the new carpet. May said I did it on purpose so I would not be asked to do it again.

We were very happy and my concert work was increasing all the time. People were asking why I wasn't on the wireless, and I used to pooh-pooh the idea and say, 'I'm not going to give away all my jokes and songs for what the BBC pays.' Deep inside me, I was longing for them to book me, but I did not seem to be able to get 'in'.

Pantomime time again, so we regretfully left our little flat and this time travelled to Leicester to appear in *Dick Whittington* at the Opera House. The first morning we had the usual read through in a room over the pub next to the theatre. Everybody read their lines – Alice, Dick, Fitzwarren, King Rat, Cheeky Sammy (me) – but when it came to the Cat, he wasn't there to do his 'Meeow'. Had he been called? Oh yes, he was called like everyone else. We kept on reading with a pause every time the Cat was mentioned. 'Are you sure he was called?' 'Certain – I can't think what has happened.' We had been reading about an hour, when the door was flung open and a tall man in a long overcoat, black homburg hat, and patent leather shoes stood in the doorway and said, 'Mornin' all – I'm Pussy'! He turned out to be a real character. All 'animals' – dog, cat, goose, etc. – had to supply their own skins. This fellow's skin had obviously been run up for him by his wife and looked like two hearthrugs sewn together. As I said, he was very tall, and the cat's head was much too small for the body. The governor caught him doing a line for himself on the side. Every interval he used to sneak through the pass-door and prowl around

B

the circle with a tin suspended round his neck, together with a notice that read 'For Pussy'! And he insisted on silver: anyone who offered to put a penny in the tin had the coin knocked out of his hand accompanied by an angry 'Meeow'. He did not last long in the pantomime.

This was to be my last pantomime for five years and also May's last appearance. My concert work was increasing all the time, and I could make more money from that than by appearing in a provincial pantomime, and I could also live at home. I spent the next two summer seasons at Margate (concert work was negligible during the summer months) and life was really wonderful.

When at Margate I used to swim at Palm Bay and play golf nearly every day and I took the twice-daily show in my stride. I had started to write my own songs and even some of my jokes were original, but I still could not get a BBC engagement. I had tentative enquiries about playing the Music Halls, but the money they offered did not attract me. Taking into account the travelling, the digs, and the agent's commission, I was better off in the concert world. And quite frankly, I was scared of the Halls. When I used to watch the George Robeys and Max Millers doing their acts, I thought to myself 'That is something I could never do.' And I was no shrinking violet. It was just that I felt I did not have the attack, or the material, the Music Hall performers seemed to have. Mind you, I was not averse to using their gags. Many is the time that I popped into the Holborn Empire and 'knocked off' some star comedian's jokes, and repeated them at a Masonic a few minutes later! I once came unstuck at a dinner at the Grosvenor House Hotel. I had seen Tex McLeod at the Holborn and he always opened his act by saying, 'I hope you are going to laugh at me, 'cos I had a peep at you through the curtains before I came on, and I had a damn good laugh at you!' I went on and cracked this gag, and when I had finished my turn, I went into the artistes' room and there was the surprise star artiste – Tex McLeod. And he had heard me! He was announced, went on to do his turn, and started with the gag I had already told. He got a big laugh with it too. I was standing watching him from the side and he turned to me and said, 'If you are going to pinch a gag, see you crack it properly!'

The Concert Artists' Association had its Club premises over the

Leicester Square Tube Station. I was proposed by Fred Wildon and joined in 1926. For the following few years I spent many happy hours there. In my early days at the Club, I used to love rubbing shoulders with the Western Brothers, Clapham and Dwyer, Norman Long, Leonard Henry, and all the big names who were heard on the wireless so much at that time. Late in the evening the place would be crowded with tenors, baritones, sopranos, contraltos, entertainers, comedians and instrumentalists – all in evening dress, having appeared at their various functions. The usual 'pro' chat like 'How well I did at Frascati's,' or 'What a terrible pianist at the Monico,' or 'I did four shows tonight – fitted them all in easily,' would abound. This was the problem, fitting in times. I have set out to do three or four engagements all carefully timed, on paper. I would arrive at the Park Lane to be told 'Oh, they were late sitting down to dinner,' so would then dash off to the Connaught Rooms where they would be on time and you were told 'You follow this speech' and some fellow would talk for half an hour. Then back to the Park Lane, where they were still not ready for you, so you would hurry off to Cannon Street, where you were asked why you were late! But I am certain that in my eighteen years of after-dinner entertaining, coupled with concerts and cabarets, I never let anybody down – timewise, at any rate.

Another great snag was the pianist, usually the man who booked you. It was a joy to arrive at a function and find a professional accompanist waiting to play for you. I used to sing a lot of medleys which involved changes of tempo and key, and I have often had to push an indifferent pianist off his stool and finish up playing for myself. And as most of the pianos were on the floor – not on the usual small platform – I used to diasppear from sight and 'lose' my audience. As soon as I could afford it in the middle thirties, I used to take my own pianist Eric Fowler around with me and save myself a lot of headaches. I remember giving my music to a Lodge organist on one occasion – it was manuscript and he told me he couldn't play 'home-made music'!

At most functions, we were asked 'what we would have' and there were usually sandwiches as well as drinks. At the more posh affairs, if there were four or five artistes, there would be a bottle of whisky and a bottle of gin. I'm afraid some of the performers used to carry medicine bottles in their music cases and 'top' up to take away drink, in addition to what they drank on the premises. One concertina player had a case that held three instruments, though he only played two. The empty compartment was duly filled with sandwiches and drink when he packed up after doing his turn. The male artistes were often offered cigars varying from Coronas to what I used to call 'Masonic Bonfires'. I never was a cigar smoker, but I always accepted one 'to smoke later'. I made quite a collection during the winter months, and I used to 'grade' them and send them off to my father, who loved a cigar.

My last season at Margate was in 1929. I had received enquiries from several concert party proprietors who seemed anxious to offer me an engagement. The two that attracted me most were George Royle and Greatrex Newman's 'Fol-de-Rols', which had shows at Scarborough, Eastbourne, and Hastings, and Powis Pinder's 'Sunshine' Concert Party at the Summer Theatre, Shanklin. During my two visits to Ventnor with 'Song Salad', I had heard of the wonderful show that the Pinders presented at their cosy little theatre. So when Mrs ('Momma') Pinder came to see me at Margate – and evidently liked what she saw – she offered me the job for the following year at the same salary I was receiving at Margate, eighteen pounds a week. It also had the added incentive of a 'benefit'. This meant that I was given all of the takings for one night towards the end of the season which, she said, usually worked out at around one hundred pounds. And there were no matinées – just six extra Sunday shows at the height of the season. Mrs Pinder warned me that I would be following a comedian-entertainer named Edwin (Teddy) Styles who was a terrific favourite in the Isle of Wight, and had been for the past nine years. And she also pointed out that he was everything that I was not – tall, good-looking, suave, witty, etc., which gave me cause to ponder!

Anyway, I said I would let her know and after a chat with Fred Wildon, who was most understanding, I wrote off and accepted the eighteen-week engagement. Back in London, I was busier than ever in the concert world and at long last, I was employed by the BBC. They used to do what were known as Empire Broadcasts to Australia, New Zealand, Canada, etc., and as they were done live, it meant I was in the studios and broadcasting somewhere around

3 a.m. for a fee of about three guineas. But what did I care: I could now put on my brochures 'The popular BBC comedian'!

With things developing the way they were, May and I moved into a new flat at 3 Exchange Mansions, Golders Green Road. It was only some five hundred yards from the old flat, but was much 'grander' (we thought) and cost another pound a week. I also bought my first car, second-hand for a hundred pounds, from an old friend of mine called Walter Allkins. The car was an Essex – Terraplane – a big American job which had a radiator that looked like a Rolls. Walter had treated it like a child, and it really was in superb condition. He taught me to drive it and sternly told me how to look after it in every way.

My mother, father, and sister decided they would like to come and live in London to be near their talented relative, so I bought them a house in Finchley. They had, of course, spent their summer holidays at Margate while I was there and I visited them in Liverpool whenever I had a break. I did not tell them I had bought a car and when I drove up there in it, it caused great consternation among the neighbours who all thought it was a Rolls – as I had hoped. I could hear 'He must be doing well' on all sides, and my mother's pride knew no bounds. We drove to her birthplace and visited the grave of her parents in Hartford Cemetery. She almost invited them to pop out of their resting-place to have a look at my car! They moved to their new home shortly afterwards, so now the entire Askey Clan was domiciled in London. Father had retired at the age of fifty-five – much too young with his ability, but he seemed quite content to live on his investments. My sister found a job as a shorthand-typist and Mother, as always, was the complete housewife.

I did not regret missing out on pantomime that winter, but I did miss the atmosphere. There was, and still is, something about pantomime that I love. It is a great family affair and it's marvellous to hear the reactions from the kiddies. I always have said that a pantomime is not a pantomime unless the theatre smells of oranges and children's wee-wee! Of course, in those days, the children were enchanted with the whole thing. Nowadays the little blighters are more sophisticated, or shall I say, undisciplined. I used to throw sweets out into the audience and they were more than gratefully received. Now the little darlings will chuck them back at you! So much for the Welfare State. When I did my undressing scene as Dame, I used to get yells of laughter from the kids; now I remove my many petticoats to the accompaniment of wolf-whistles and cries of 'Get 'em off!'

The winter months passed quickly and it was now time to pre-pare again for the summer season with the Pinders at Shanklin. We were called for rehearsals at a hotel in Bloomsbury where we used the Ballroom, and I met my new guv'nor, Powis Pinder, for the first time. He was a most charming man, and he and 'Momma' Pinder had both been in the Gilbert and Sullivan Operas with the original D'Oyly Carte Company. He used to tell me wonderful stories about going to Sullivan's flat in Artillery Mansions, Victoria, and hearing those lovely songs for the first time. He was never a 'star', but played all the 'bit' parts, as did Ethel ('Momma'), his wife.

Rehearsals went very smoothly and I found my new colleagues very delightful and most talented. The company was about twelve in number, and one of the features of the Sunshine Company was was the way the show was dressed. Each girl had at least four frocks and 'Momma' used to spend a fortune on them. I would have said the expense nearly turned 'Poppa's' hair grey, but he wore a wig. He had two as a matter of fact, an auburn one for when he was feeling skittish, and one flecked with grey when he was worried. But 'Poppa' and 'Momma' Pinder, together with their son Arthur, were delightful people with whom I was to spend the following eight summers, the happiest days of my life.

ANTHEA'S DEBUT

THE SUNSHINE COMPANY was a real family set-up. 'Poppa' Pinder was the compère of the actual show, took part occasionally in the sketches, and invariably forgot his words. 'Momma' was in the box-office and was a genius in the way she manipulated the seats. She could always tell if it was going to rain in the evening by the clouds over Luccombe Chine, and the seats in the theatre would be adjusted accordingly. The family atmosphere was completed by young Arthur Pinder, who was the stage manager.

Apart from her wizardry in the box-office, 'Momma' was a tremendous asset to the show with her wonderful laugh. She reserved a permanent seat for herself and once the patrons were all inside the theatre, she would take her seat and roar her head off at every funny line I cracked. Her timing was not always perfect and often the laugh would come before I had actually got the gag out! But she was a dear; the Pinders were marvellous, and so were their shows.

Our opposition was the show at the Pier Pavilion. During the eight years I was at Shanklin, Clarkson Rose, Ronald Frankau, Rupert Hazell, and my old mate Tommy Trinder appeared there at different times – but I saw them all off! It was very funny in the evenings to see Mrs Pinder looking at the Pier entrance with a pair of binoculars to see if they had the 'House Full' sign out, while Mrs Terry Wood, the Pier proprietor's wife, was doing the same thing to see how we were faring. I can honestly say that we were always full to capacity all the time I was there, and the theatre seated six hundred.

Artistes in the show whose names might be familiar to some of you were Webster Booth, Raymond Newell, Mario de Pietro, and Bernard Lee – 'M' in the recent James Bond films. And the pianist for all the eight years was Kathleen O'Hagan, who was the wife of my old friend and pianist Sydney Jerome. And what happy shows they were. I usually managed a round of golf every morning, a swim in the afternoon, and an occasional game of tennis, and then the greatest pleasure of all, the show at night.

The first time I met David Niven, he told me it was through me that he ever went into show business. His people had a house at Bembridge, where the family spent the summer months. David used to visit the Summer Theatre two or three times every week and he thought I looked so happy in my work, he resolved that it would be 'An actor's life for me'! Or should I say 'him'? When he told me this, I suggested he paid me a small commission for putting the idea into his head, but he didn't put his money where his mouth was. One well-known West End actress who used to disport herself on the Shanklin beach was Heather Thatcher – the only person I ever saw who bathed wearing a monocle. And a costume, I hasten to add.

Saturday was the night for the local celebrities, who included Sir John Martin Harvey, the novelist H. de Vere Stacpoole, Lord St Vincent, Lord Jellicoe, The Comtesse di Sibour, the Hon. this, Lady that – quite a social gathering. They frequently sent up 'requests' for various songs and sketches when they brought friends to see the show. I felt I was moving into high society at last.

I played golf several times with the ex-Admiral of the Fleet, Lord Jellicoe of Jutland. He was very deaf – probably caused by the big guns – and I used to have to shout at him to make myself heard. I often arrived at the theatre in the evening almost speechless. I also played with a Mr Fox, who was a great botanist and naturalist. He had the habit of pausing during his very slow back swing, dropping his club, picking up something he saw growing, and saying, 'Now this is something you don't often see on this side of the Island!' I thought at first he was referring to my golf!

My 'benefit' reaped me the hundred pounds I had been promised as well as an assortment of ties, handkerchiefs, cigars, bottles of whisky, flowers, etc. from admirers, so I knew I had made a good impression with the Shanklin visitors and residents. I was not surprised to be invited back for the following season at twenty pounds a week, a rise of two pounds. In the last week of the season we visited various towns on the island: Ryde, Ventnor, Newport, etc., finishing up at the Summer Theatre on the Saturday with the usual feelings of sadness and relief.

During the season, I had been receiving letters booking me for various functions and by the time I returned home, I had quite a full diary. I had no thought of a break for years, for I always imagined my summers at the seaside constituted a holiday, so once again I started dashing around between the Connaught Rooms, the Holborn Restaurant (gone), Frascati's (gone), the Monico, Anderton's, Pinoli's, etc. – all gone too now. But I was also doing some of the better functions at the Grosvenor House, the Dorchester, the Savoy, the Café Royal, and other 'posh' venues. Like all the other artistes who were away in summer shows, I announced my return in *The Sunday Referee* (gone!) as follows:

ARTHUR   ASKEY

Returns to Town October 5th

Address until that date –

SUMMER THEATRE, SHANKLIN.

(Where I return next Season)

SUNDAY, SEPT. 28th – PALLADIUM and Croydon Hippodrome
(N.S.L.)

So the winter season of 1931 to 1932 passed pleasantly and profitably and in no time at all I was heading off for Shanklin again. There were a few changes in the cast, but again everybody was very pleasant, and we had the same wonderful governors – the Pinders. I received a great welcome back and my cup of joy overflowed when I took May to see Dr Cowper and he confirmed she was going to have a baby! We had postponed the idea of becoming parents until I was sure my touring days were over. Now with my London concert connections, and an annual summer season, we knew where we stood in the dicey world of entertainment.

Therefore 1933 was a lucky year for me. My daughter, Anthea, was born on 2 March, and I had my tonsils removed by the same doctor in the same nursing home – a sort of package deal. In the same year I was booked for my first real radio appearance in *John Sharman's Music Hall*, a very popular show broadcast every Satur-day night. I trembled with excitement as I signed the contract for five guineas and had it witnessed (the rule in those days) by Tom Kinniburgh, the bass, with whom I was appearing on the evening of the contract's arrival. The bill for *Music Hall*, published in the *Radio Times* for 17 February, was as follows:

FLORENCE OLDHAM
Syncopated Songs at the Piano

ARTHUR ASKEY
Entertainer

JANET JOYE
Burlesque Impersonations, with Blandford Collin
at the piano

CHICK FARR
Assisted by Bert Farland

HENRI LEONI
The Anglo-French Singer

JULIAN ROSE
Our Hebrew Friend

THE B.B.C. THEATRE ORCHESTRA
Under the direction of S. Kneale Kelley
will play during the programme

I was so nervous that night, I didn't take my car to Broadcasting House but went by tube to Oxford Circus. The streets were crowded with people as I walked to the BBC and I remember thinking with

relief, 'At least these people won't be home in time to hear me.'
How defeatist can you get! John Sharman, for whom I worked a
great deal later on and whom I christened 'The Great Ziegfeld',
did not make things easier. He was very fussy and 'important', and
cut my time from eight minutes to five, just as I was going on.
However, I seemed to do all right. Collie Knox, the much-feared
radio critic in the *Daily Mail*, wrote: 'Arthur Askey, a newcomer
to the air, proved himself a comedian of resource. He got over well.'
I made one gaffe during rehearsals. I listened to Julian Rose, a very
funny Jewish comedian, go through his act with gags like 'My wife
and I were in a motor accident the other day; neither of us was
hurt, but fortunately I had the presence of mind to kick her in the
face. I received the insurance money this morning.' I said to him
(toady that I was), 'I think you'd do wonderfully in America, Mr
Rose.' He looked at me and said, 'Son – I *am* an American!'

Another happy season at Shanklin followed, where the Askey
baby received a great deal of attention. Anthea was christened at
St Saviour's-on-the-Cliff with Mrs Pinder acting as godmother.
Anthea's name was inspired by a song that Webster Booth used
to sing in the show. My wife had wanted to call our new offspring
'Ann' but I pointed out that 'Ann Askey' somehow sounded
illiterate, so we thought of Anita, Annabelle, etc. and I suddenly
remembered 'Boothy' announcing his song 'To Anthea', which was
a poem by Ben Jonson set to music. We decided it was a nice name,
so Anthea Shirley was duly christened on 30 July 1933, by the
Rev. Montague Bere. The church was crowded with the entire
Sunshine cast and many of the locals and visitors, so Anthea
opened to a full house!

During the season, my old pantomime boss, Fred Clements, came
down to see me and asked me if I would appear for him again in
Babes in the Wood at the Theatre Royal, Nottingham, at Christmas.
This time I was to be the star and he offered me forty pounds a
week. As I was appearing at most of the same functions in London
each winter and was finding new material more difficult to obtain,
I decided to accept his offer. I suppose the reason I was finding it
harder to get new jokes was the fact that I was so busy, I didn't get
the chance to nip into the Music Halls and pinch material from my
more famous colleagues! But I had time on returning to London to

do quite a number of concerts before starting rehearsals for pantomime.

I remember I appeared at the Grosvenor House for a Motor Trades dinner and Sir Alfred (later Lord) Austin was in the chair. Sir William Morris (later Lord Nuffield) was also at the top table, together with the heads of all the various car companies. At that time I was cracking a gag where I did a cod cough and said to the audience, 'If you have to smoke, I hope you are smoking Player's. I merely mention that because last week as I was appearing at a dinner I mentioned Player's cigarettes, and there happened to be a director of John Player's in the audience. And do you know, two days later, I received a thousand Player's cigarettes for giving them a plug. A few nights later, I happened to mention Johnny Walker at another dinner – there was a director in the audience – and two days later, I received a case of Johnny Walker.' I looked around the room, full of the heads of the various motor car manufacturers, and said, 'I still think the Austin is the finest car in the world!' Later in the artistes' room, Sir William Morris walked in and he said to me, 'If you had said that Morris was the best car in the world, you would have had a Morris car delivered to your door, with my compliments. You won't get a bloody spanner from Austin!'

Came December and I packed my bags to travel to rehearsals at Nottingham. I rather regretted leaving May and our new baby, but thought I'd get back for a few hours at Christmas by hook or by crook. We opened the pantomime on Christmas Eve, the show went very well and, at last, I was in Number 1 dressing room in a major theatre.

Christmas Day dawned, but there was no way of telling it had. Snow and ice lay round about, accompanied by thick fog, and my chances of getting home to London were obviously nil. Even if I had managed it, what about the matinée on Boxing Day? So I phoned May, who cried when I told her the news. She let Anthea gurgle into the phone, which completed my sense of misery. I was staying in what was laughingly described as a 'Temperance Hotel' and the clientele was one hundred per cent commercial travellers. The proprietor's office was just inside the hallway and it was impossible to pass the door without being hauled in to 'have one'! When I got back from the theatre each night, I tried walking on tip-toe and closing the door quietly, but he'd hear me and insist I meet his friends – old and new – and 'have one' with him. He would then regale the assembled company with stories of his great days 'on the boards' and say how sorry he felt for youngsters like me in the 'profession'!

On this Christmas Day, he was well drunk by midday – as were all of the staff – and I was the only guest in the hotel. The one ancient waiter who was still able to stagger brought me turkey, roast potatoes, and sprouts – stone cold, but with warm gravy – and left me in the large dining room all alone. It was like a scene from Dickens and it would be an understatement for me to say I was just miserable. The fellow who was playing Dame in the panto was Charlie Harrison. He and his wife Ethel were staying in digs and Ethel had said to Charlie, 'I'll bet Arthur hasn't been able to get home. Pop around and see.' So Charlie walked, or rather skated, to the hotel, looked through the window, and saw the forlorn figure of A.A. going through the motions of eating his Christmas dinner. He entered the hotel and quietly opened the dining room door. I heard the noise, looked round and said to him, 'And a Merry Christmas to you, too!' We laughed about it for many years after. Anyway, I went back with him to his digs and spent a reasonably happy Christmas. But my thoughts were with my little wife and our baby. And I swore we would never spend another Christmas apart – not even for fifty pounds a week.

May came up to see the pantomime, arrived with raging 'flu, spent four days in bed and then hurried back to Anthea, not having seen the genius at work.

During the run of the pantomime, Horace Reeves of Reeves and Lamport, then the biggest agents for booking artistes on the Music Halls, came to see the show. He said he thought I would do well on the Halls and suggested he should start booking me some dates. When he asked what money he should ask for me, I told him I would want a hundred pounds a week and to be top of the bill. He laughed and asked me how on earth I hoped to achieve it. I had to admit I had no idea, but my demands would somehow have to be met. Deep inside me, I was scared of playing the Halls, but I didn't tell him so. I did say, however, that if the time did arrive when I deigned to become a Music Hall performer, I would give him the first refusal, topping the bill at one hundred pounds a week. He said it could never happen. I hoped to prove him wrong.

The panto over, I returned to London and a lot of bookings for various concerts, plus the odd broadcast. I was also asked if I would take part in some experimental broadcasts in the afternoons, at a fee of two guineas. I found myself staring into a bright light with moving lines passing 'before my very eyes'. I was repeatedly asked to constrict my movements and keep my hands close to my face, instead of flailing them about as I usually did. The whole thing seemed to me to be very Heath Robinson and I could see no future in it. In this instance it was me that was wrong. I was 'in' at the birth of television.

In no time at all, we were packing for my fifth season at Shanklin where my money had risen to thirty pounds a week, as befitted a 'well-known BBC entertainer'! Clarkson Rose was the opposition on the Pier that season. He asked me to meet him one day and he told me that he had asked Julian Wylie (whose pantomime I had seen in rehearsal at Liverpool) to come to Shanklin and see me work. Wylie had a new musical he wanted to produce and he wanted a comedian who was a cross between Leslie Henson and Bobby Howes. I was very excited about this, especially when 'Clarkie' told me that Wylie was coming to see me the following Saturday in the company of Ernest Edelston, a very well-known agent. I suppose it was a case of the usual show biz story: I knew they were in front and instead of working normally, I 'tried' too hard. Or perhaps they just didn't think I was funny. Anyway, the following morning they returned to the mainland and didn't even offer me the part of understudy. Perhaps Wylie remembered me as the phoney from the School Attendance office!

However, the Pinders still thought I was good and booked me again for the following season. I had received quite a number of offers from different managements, some at a bigger salary, but I was very happy at Shanklin and with the entire set-up there.

I naturally had to find new songs every season, though there were often requests for the old ones – I saw to that! I was walking through Leicester Square one day and bumped into another Liverpool comedian called Kenneth Blain. He was working at the Windmill Theatre, a soul-destroying job if ever there was one, and he said he had written a song he thought would suit me. There and then he sang me a verse and chorus of 'The Bee'. I liked it and paid him two guineas for the summer rights to sing it at Shanklin. When I came back to London I asked him if I could use it in my concert work; he agreed, and another two guineas changed hands. I found I was constantly being asked to sing the song, so continued to pay Kenneth a couple of guineas for the privilege. He was pleased to take my money, but not so pleased that I was making a success of his own brain-child. He told me he had tried it in his act, but it meant nothing to the audience. Actually I had had to drop it in pantomime at Nottingham in 1933, it didn't go well at all. But in concert party and Masonics, it was a riot.

When we commenced *Band Waggon* on radio, I used to include a song every week but thought 'The Bee' had to be seen to be appreciated. When I performed it I used to dash around the stage with my arms and dress-suit tails flying and I thought that was what made it such a success. However, one week I was stuck for a song for *Band Waggon* so I included 'The Bee'. It was an instant hit and I received dozens, even hundreds, of letters asking me to repeat it on the air. And it has stuck with me ever since; it has been published and I have recorded it at least three times, so Kenneth made quite a bit of money out of it, apart from what I paid him through the years. But he resented the fact that *he* couldn't get it over in his performance all the same. He was a fine writer, almost in the Gilbert and Sullivan class. I sang most of his songs – 'The Moth', 'Chirrup Chirrup', 'The Flea', 'Pretty Little Bird', etc. – and I also used his eccentric monologues 'Picture if you can, a winkle' and 'When the Captain hung his whiskers out to dry'. When I had exhausted his repertoire, I started writing my own songs, much in the same vein: 'The Seagull', 'The Worm', 'The Mosquito', and several others. But 'The Bee' remains the daddy of them all and I always end my act to this day by saying to the audience, 'When I was in *Band Waggon* I always sang little songs about insects or birds, well, tonight I'm going to sing the original of all these silly little songs. Guess what it's called?' Invariably they shout 'The Bee', so God bless you, Kenneth Blain – dead now, but not forgotten by a grateful comic.

This reminds me of the first time I bought a comic song which in comparison to the success of 'The Bee' must have been my all-time failure. It was back in my first season at Brighton with 'Song Salad'. I was an avid reader of *The Stage* at the time, and in the advertising columns under the heading 'Authors and Composers' I had noticed that 'Percival Langley – Writer to the Stars' lived in Brighton. Well, in search of some original songs I presented myself at the composer's residence which, although sounding grand in print, turned out to be a seedy terraced house in a run-down suburb. An unkempt landlady directed me to Langley's rooms, where I was received by the maestro himself, freshly awakened. His appearance blended harmoniously with the dingy room, unmade bed, and the ancient upright piano. This did not really upset me; after all Bach wrote some of his finest music in a garret. Mr Langley sat at the piano in his dressing gown, and proceeded to render some of his compositions. This was hampered by the cigarette dangling from his lips, which often caused some of the words to be disguised by bouts of turbulent coughing.

I heard about twenty songs and decided to take one called 'I've got nothing much to do'. It was about a henpecked husband who did all the domestic chores. My choice was influenced by the composer, who said it was the best song he had ever written and would 'paralyse' my audience. Also I could have the world rights for two guineas – a special price as I was a beginner in the business. That night I performed the song at the Aquarium, Brighton, and as you might guess nobody laughed, not even the fish. However, the 'Writer to the Stars' was right, his song certainly 'paralysed' my audience.

I seem to be moving through my early years quickly, but I assure you that in detail they would easily make an encyclopedia! We are now in the winter of 1934 and back in London for a round of concerts. More and more, I was appearing at posh affairs, even at the Albert Hall, Queens Hall, and the like. I was also being booked for provincial functions by the leading agents. I usually found myself in the company of some of the country's leading singers and instrumentalists.

I remember one occasion when I was booked for three nights at the Gladstone Liberal Club in Barnoldswick in Yorkshire. There were four top singers and myself and we all appeared three times

Above: On stage with Dickie Murdoch.
Left: The Palladium programme, 1939.

Top: From the 'Band Waggon' film: Stinker taking me off.

Bottom: In 'Jack and Jill' at the Palace Theatre, London, with Eddie Gray.

Opposite: Charley's 'Big-hearted' Aunt.

Above: At Scapa Flow with Jack Hylton and Sir Bruce Fraser.

Right: Typical wartime performance at the Nuffield Centre.

on each of the three nights, making nine separate performances. And the vocalists sang duets and even trios on occasion – such singers as Peter Dawson, Lenghi Cellini, tenor, Clara Serena, contralto, and Olive Groves, soprano. I was so successful that I was engaged for the following year and had to find jokes and songs for another nine appearances! The Club itself was a real piece of Victoriana, with gas footlights and the front of the stage surrounded by huge palms and aspidistras. They had to remove a lot of them so I could be seen, especially when I sat down at the piano.

I did a concert at Consett, Co. Durham, on another occasion. The fee was about fifteen guineas, plus train fare and 'hospitality'. This meant you could stay the night with the vicar or the doctor or some local big-wig. My host was very pleasant and lived in a rather large but gloomy Victorian detached house. On arrival I went up to my bedroom to hang up 'my frock' and get sorted out. There was a tap on the door and the housekeeper-maid shuffled in. She was a rather frowsy-looking woman and from under her apron she produced a shoe-horn and said 'Norman Long's'. She crept out, returning a few minutes later with a clothes brush, and said 'Leonard Henry's'. These were two of the entertainers who had stayed at the house previously, so I took no chances. When I went off to do the concert, I took everything with me. And when I left in the morning, I double-checked that I had everything. It was not until I got to the station that I realised that I had left my overcoat hanging in the hall overnight, and that next year's entertainer would be shown 'Arthur Askey's gloves'!

I returned to London on the train with Dennis Noble, a fine baritone who had been on the bill with me. At lunchtime we walked along the corridor to the dining car and passed a first-class compartment where we saw a huddled figure sitting alone with his feet up on the seat, wrapped in an overcoat with an astrakhan collar. Dennis whispered in awed tones, 'It's Sir Thomas Beecham.' He turned back and kept passing and repassing the corridor window, but there was no response from Sir Thomas, who had his eyes tightly closed. After lunch, we walked back past the compartment and there was the great man in exactly the same position. Beecham, of course, had a lot of influence in the engaging of singers for his concerts, and Dennis was determined to be noticed in case the

F

conductor should be wanting a baritone in the near future. He again hovered by the window and eventually slid the door open and said 'Why, hello Sir Thomas – how are you?' Beecham opened his eyes and shouted, 'Terrible! Shut that bloody door.' I don't think Dennis ever sang for him again. Personally, I never worked for Beecham, but I admit that his family's products have sometimes worked for me!

In 1936 we were on the move again to a larger flat (two bathrooms, no less) in Windsor Court, about half a mile from Exchange Mansions and still in Golders Green. The rent was four pounds a week inclusive and I had a garage for my car – an Austin 16. We also had a maid at one pound a week, so I was moving into the luxury class. Anthea started school at La Sagesse Convent, which was just around the corner, and I had mentally settled down to a routine of concert party and concerts and was feeling very pleased with life.

BIRTH OF BAND WAGGON

I HAD SIGNED for a further summer season at my beloved Shanklin and my diary was full of concert dates. I was also getting into the night-club scene. Ronald Frankau had rung me and asked if I could do a Friday night for him at the 'Cosmo Club' in Wardour Street. He was booked there for the week, but had an odd date to fill at Cambridge and the management told him they would release him if he could find a deputy for the one night. I knew that Ronnie's material was rather on the 'blue' side and wondered if my concert party patter and songs would stand up to the night-club audience's requirements. I had no need to worry for I was very successful, so much so that I was booked for a week. I was then offered three weeks at the 'Trianon' in Jermyn Street following its opening. The first night was packed, everything being free, but the business afterwards was very indifferent. In fact, some nights I didn't show at all, but as it didn't affect my wages I was not unduly worried.

My next night-club engagement was at 'Chez Henri' in Long Acre. I opened on the Monday night but soon realised I was not right for this particular audience. One member sat right in front of me and read his evening paper during the whole of my act. I made witty (?) references to him while I was working, but they didn't make any impression on him, or the rest of the audience for that matter. The following morning I received a phone call asking me not to bother to turn up for the rest of the week and I decided there and then that night-clubs were not for me, for the present time anyway.

In late May of 1936 we were off to Shanklin again and staying at the Medehamsted Hotel – very posh, and costing me all of eight guineas a week for the three of us. My salary was now thirty-five pounds a week and we had also let our London flat at six pounds a week, so we could afford to splash out a little. After our usual happy and successful season, it was back to London and the concert routine. I felt I was becoming really famous, but had a slight set-back when I was asked to do the Green Room Rag at the Vaude-ville Theatre one Sunday night. *The Times* said on the following day:

> The greatest success was scored by a substitute who took a place in the programme without notice. MR. ARTHUR ASKEW, apparently bearing up gallantly under a desperate gaucherie, but actually master of a curious double-barrelled humour, which drowned every titter with a roar.

Although I didn't quite understand what the critic meant, I was naturally delighted but I did wish he had got my name right. I was now definitely King of the Concert World and did well at nearly all of my shows. There was an occasional Waterloo however: for in-stance, in the December of that year on the night the King abdi-cated. I was booked for a Masonic ladies' night at the Clarendon, Hammersmith. After the meal and a couple of speeches, a wireless set was wheeled into the room and switched on so that the assembled company could hear the abdication speech about 'giving up my throne to go away with the woman I love' etc. As you can well imagine, when H.R.H. had finished his speech, there was not a dry eye in the ballroom of the Clarendon. The worshipful Master managed to announce through his sobs, 'You are now to be enter-tained by Mr Arthur Askey.' Mr Arthur Askey knew he hadn't got a hope in hell – it was the longest twenty minutes of my life. When

I'd finished I joined in the sobs myself, but for a different reason. I hadn't got one laugh!

My next new experience in the entertainment business was my first appearance in a film. B. C. Hilliam (Flotsam of Flotsam and Jetsam) had told me there was a part for me in a new film to be made called *Calling All Stars*. This was to feature Ambrose and his Band, and a galaxy of popular entertainers including of course Flotsam and Jetsam. I contacted British Lion Films and was asked to attend Beaconsfield Studios for one day's shooting. I was to play the part of a waiter. Naturally, this was somewhat deflating, but like everyone else I was dying to get into films and this seemed like a big opportunity. I arrived promptly at 8 a.m. on the appropriate day with my own dress suit and tie, and was assured that as I had six Masonics that night, I would be away from the studios at 6 p.m.

The scene in which I was to 'feature' involved my approaching a table in a restaurant at which sat several celebrities, including Davy Burnaby (who appeared with the Co-Optimists), and indulging in some waiter jokes with Davy, which would conclude with an introduction to the next act. Well, I asked for a script and was promptly requested to write down any waiter jokes I might know. I went up to my dressing room and wrote about four pages of witty waiter dialogue such as:

'Waiter, do you serve lobsters?'
'Yes sir, sit down – we serve anybody!'
'I'm so hungry, I could eat a horse.'
'We've only got the doovers.'
'What doovers?'
'The horse's doovers.'
'Have you any fresh salmon?'
'I think it will be fresh, sir!'
'What do you mean, you think it will be fresh?'
'Well, we won't know until we open the tin!'
'Have you a wild duck?'
'No, sir, but I've got a tame one I could aggravate for you.'

Every one a little gem!! It was now about 10 a.m.; I had changed into my waiter's outfit and hung around the set clutching my precious manuscript. The morning crept on and I was fascinated watching the filming of Ambrose and his Band and various acts, singers and musicians, all well known on the radio and Music Halls. There was the usual lunch break and still I had not been called to do my big scene. Filming recommenced after lunch and by late afternoon I was beginning to get worried about my evening engagements. Eventually I was called to make my début in films. They slapped some make-up on me, gave me a serviette to hang over my arm, and we were set for a take. Before any action took place, however, I was asked to remove my glasses. I pleaded that they were part of my image, but with the quick rebuff 'Take 'em off, son, you don't see waiters wearing glasses,' they duly disappeared. I delivered my dialogue, which sounded less funny as the afternoon wore on, collected my fee (ten pounds), and rapidly left the studio only just in time for my evening appointments. At least I thought the foundations of a career in films might have been laid.

Some weeks later a couple of tickets arrived for the trade showing of the picture. It was to be held at the Piccadilly Theatre. I was working as usual and could not go, but my wife went with a friend. I rushed home after I had finished my shows and found May at home, laughing her head off. Success, I thought, Hollywood here I come. However, she explained to me that halfway through the epic, a figure she didn't recognise (me without my glasses) walked up to a table and Davy Burnaby said to him, 'Who's appearing in the Cabaret tonight, waiter?' and the unrecognisable waiter replied, 'Why, the four Marvellos'!! All those lovely jokes were on the cutting-room floor. Ah well, that's show business, I suppose.

However, there was some compensation, as Pathé Films asked me if I would appear in their Pathé Pictorial. This was a very popular magazine-type film which was shown on most circuits and usually concluded with a four- or five-minute spot by a well-known entertainer. I went along to the little studio in Wardour Street, donned my evening dress, funny hat, and white gloves, told a couple of gags and went into 'The Bee' song. A week later it was being shown at the News Reel Theatre in Piccadilly, so naturally I went along to see 'me'. The theatre was full and when I came on the screen, I received quite a lot of laughs and I felt very pleased with myself. I was wearing a new dress suit in the film which had cost me all of six guineas, and I was just thinking how smart I looked when a woman behind me said to her friend, 'He's deformed, isn't he?'!! And the film wasn't even out of focus!

Reflecting on my life at this time, I could not have been more content. I was now thirty-six years old and had successfully accomplished the troublesome starting years of a career in show business. There were still hurdles to be overcome, but fortunately with my height I felt I could run beneath them! At least with my established summer season and concert dates in London, I was not running around the country like most people in the profession. In addition, my domestic life with my May and my daughter Anthea was perfect. This is how I wanted my life to go on.

After every summer season, my first visit to the theatre was to see my adored Leslie Henson, who usually produced a new musical comedy about September each year. I had reconciled myself to the fact that I could never filch his job, but little did I know that in a few weeks' time – at Christmas to be exact – I would be starring in a West End theatre in a musical. Only a children's play, but nevertheless, a musical.

The Boy Who Lost His Temper was written by Mrs Rica Bromley Taylor, and the music was by Geoffrey Henman. The story of the play was told very concisely in *The Times*' notice:

> The story concerns a certain nine year old boy, Keith by name, whose temper is his strong characteristic. Father, mother, nurse, and aunt attempt in their various ways to manage him, but his own self-will is triumphant against solo and concerted efforts until the imps from Temperland visit his bedroom and leave with his temper. Then Keith, minus temper, becomes an unutterable little prig with whom it is even more difficult to live than it was in the temper days, and a family party set out for Temperland in order to discover and obtain the boy's lost temper. It is not exactly the bad old temper that is recovered, but something more compatible with the family spirit, and we leave Keith as the host of a birthday breakfast with family and young friends all glad to enjoy the company of a happy boy. The story may sound slight as set down, but it has been handled by someone who understands

children, and it has various excursions into the fairy realms
that considerably enhance its appeal.
The note also went on to say (quite rightly!):

Arthur Askey is a joyous representative of Miss Tripaway, the
dancing mistress, Mr Teachem, the schoolmaster, and the
proprietor of Selford's Emporium. There is a breeziness about
all his work and an air of spontaneity in his humour that com-
mend themselves wholeheartedly to audiences, and he brings
the intimate touch of concert party to his impersonations,
and scores with everything that he does.

The show opened at the Garrick Theatre on 22 December and ran
to capacity business for four weeks – matinées only. And I saw my
name in large letters outside a West End Theatre for the first time.
What's more, it was spelt correctly!

So successful was the show, we repeated it the following Christmas season at the Cambridge Theatre. During rehearsals, Mrs
Bromley Taylor decided she would like to include a 'flying ballet'.
It was difficult to book Kirby's or Eugene's or any of the approved
'flying' experts as they had all long been engaged for the various
pantomimes – not to mention *Peter Pan* – up and down the country.
However, Mrs Bromley Taylor had written the play, and, I suspect,
financed it, so her wishes had to be catered for. Eventually they
found somebody who apparently knew all the tricks and mechanics
of 'flying', although he appeared with a very doubtful-looking set of
equipment which seemed as if it had belonged to Grimaldi. The
youngsters who played the Tempers (bad Tempers dressed in red,
good Tempers in white) were between ten and fourteen years of
age. Came dress rehearsal and they were strapped in their harnesses,
the stage hands were given brief instructions as to which ropes they
had to pull, and then the panic started. The kids were swung up
into the air, some sideways, some upside down, and they spun
around, banging into each other, some just off the floor, others
right up in the flies. Most of them were crying but the orchestra
played on. The ballet was supposed to be brought to an end by the
appearance of the King of Temperland. He was a large six-foot-
three bass and his entrance was to be effected by his standing on a

step-ladder in the wings and then, on cue, gliding on his wire to
the centre of the stage. He jumped off the ladder as instructed, and
fell flat on his face, while the two men holding on to the rope shot
about ten feet in the air. Needless to say, the flying ballet was cut
and the kids went back to dancing a more conventional ballet on the
stage, to the delightful music of Geoffrey Henman.

There were some very lovely songs in the show. I wrote my own
lyrics and was particularly proud of my Miss Tripaway lyric:

> I am Amelia Tripaway,
> I teach dancing every day
> Though how I make my classes pay
> Is really most surprising.
> I've to put up with the noise
> Of wayward girls and naughty boys
> But I still maintain my poise
> And stop my temper rising,
> And so throughout the day
> You'll always hear me say –
>
> Come on children, point your toe,
> Not too fast, and not too slow.
> Let your hands go to and fro,
> One two three and away we go.
> If you make the least mistake
> I'll see you through my glasses.
> Though I may be slightly faded
> I get through my work unaided,
> There's no fear of being raided
> At Tripaway's Dancing Classes.

Not quite Noël Coward, but a brave try. The point of the line
'No fear of being raided' was that at that time the police had been
busy checking up on 'Dancing Classes' where the couples had been
dancing much too close together! I think the point was missed by
the nice people with their kiddies who attended. I was paid thirty-
five pounds a week for appearing in the show (nothing for the
lyrics!) and did my usual concert work in the evenings, so my bank

manager was very happy. So was that arch-fiend the Tax Collector, who has been a regular pain in the neck.

The new King George VI was to be crowned in May, so the BBC decided to put on a big radio show called *The Coronation Revue* to celebrate the occasion. Stars of stage, films, and radio were to take part: Cicely Courtneidge, Frank Lawton, Sir Frank Benson, Harry Welchman, The Western Brothers, Revnell and West, Mabel Constanduros, Brian Lawrence, Wynne Ajello, 'Hutch', Reginald Foort, Wilson Hallett, Jack Buchanan, W. H. Berry, etc., all big stars of the day. The show was to be compèred by George Robey and Max Miller, who were to work together with a script written by Douglas Furber. When they came to rehearse, Max Miller (for me the greatest Music Hall comedian I ever saw) could not read the script. He could read all right, but was not at all happy holding the script and making it sound spontaneous. He 'bowed out' after a couple of days and I was called by John Watt, then head of Variety and Light Entertainment, who asked me if I would go and see him. After some persuasion John Watt firmly offered me the part Max Miller was to have played. The only stars I knew in the revue were Revnell & West and the Western Brothers; the others I treated with awe. I was introduced to George Robey and given the script to read through with him, and what a funny script it was. Douglas Furber had been very fair and made sure that both Robey and Max Miller got an equal share of laughs: they 'fed' each other for one gag, then got the next laugh themselves. I was cock-a-hoop on the first read through, then on the second dear old George kept saying, 'I don't think that joke suits you, son. I'd better do it!' On the next run through, he pinched still more of my lines, and I hadn't the courage to argue with him. It finished up with me doing all the straight lines. The producer was too frightened to do anything about it – George had a reputation for being awkward if he liked – so my hopes of instant stardom were being dashed at each rehearsal.

On the night of the broadcast – live, of course – I confided in my little wife and she said, 'What are you worried about, why don't you just ad lib?' I was horrified at the suggestion – me having the audacity to cross swords, as it were, with a big star. But I took her advice and when we got to the actual broadcast, I started ad libbing like a maniac. I hate to say it now, but I completely threw George, and covered myself with glory. The compliments I received after the show from all concerned (except 'The Prime Minister of Mirth') were fantastic, and at last I felt I had arrived in the first team on radio. And it was all through this that I got *Band Waggon*.

John Watt asked me to call and see him (again!). I thought he was going to give me a rocket for ad libbing because in those days if you said 'the' instead of 'but' you were hauled over the coals. I got two severe reprimands, for saying 'hell' on one occasion and 'lousy' on another. But no, he told me that the BBC was thinking of doing what they did on radio in America: having big comedy shows at a certain time on a certain night of the week.

Up to this time BBC shows were haphazard – with the possible exception of the News and *Monday Night at Seven*, which were hardly comedy shows in any event. And, he said, they were thinking (again!) about building a show around me later in the year. I got off my knees and thanked him, knowing that this was the opportunity I had been hoping for. But show business being what it is, I thought perhaps it would just be 'Promises Promises' and went back to my Masonics.

The summer came and off we went to Shanklin for what would be my last season there. I was as loath to leave the Pinders as they were loath to lose me; in fact dear 'Momma' Pinder made up a story of being left a legacy and tried to bribe me to stay on. This on top of my forty pounds a week and the hundred pounds' benefit. But I intended to quit while I was winning, though I promised to return after a season's break. I had a firm offer from Greatrex Norman for the 'Fol-de-Rols' at Hastings and I thought of all the songs, sketches, and jokes that I could use there instead of having to find new material, as I had to do for each of my eight seasons at Shanklin. But I never did do another season at Shanklin. After my season with 'The Fols' I was topping the bill at the Palladium the following summer!

Back in London, John Watt of the BBC actually did contact me about the proposed radio show. We arranged to meet at a pub, The George, near Broadcasting House. I thought this was odd considering all the space at the BBC, but gathered on John Watt's arrival that he had another comedian waiting at some other pub. He

wanted to decide between this comedian and myself. After about
ten minutes' chat he settled for me on the spot. The other fellow,
incidentally, was my old mate Dickie Hassett, who was to take my
place at Shanklin.

There was a preliminary meeting at the BBC between John Watt,
Harry S. Pepper and Gordon Crier (the producers), a scriptwriter,
Freddie Birtwell (to be my straight man), and myself.

We discussed things in the normal way, and decided to call the
show *Band Waggon*. There was a popular radio show in America at
that time called *The Band Wagon* but the difference was that in the
American show the accent was on the Band, and here it was to be
on comedy, we hoped. Harry Pepper drew five lines on a piece of
paper and after about five minutes he came up with the words and
music of the *Band Waggon* signature tune which would sweep the
country in a few weeks' time. The show was to run an hour, the
writer produced the script, we read it through, and that was the
last we saw of Freddie Birtwell. He sent a message the following day
saying he had the offer of a part in a film, but I knew why he'd
opted out. The script was not too good, and that's being kind.
However, always optimistic, I thought that with my great talent,
charm, and ad libbing, I could make it sound good. But meantime
we had to find another straight man. Gordon Crier said he knew
just the fellow, this chap was everything I wasn't – the complete
contrast. Tall, handsome, Charterhouse and Cambridge educated,
he had just finished in a show at the Saville Theatre with Stanley
Lupino, and his name – Richard Murdoch. And that, my dear
grandchildren, is how I first met 'Stinker'. We took to each other
right away; the chemistry was right. He also had ideas and we decided on the features for *Band Waggon*. Dickie and I were to do
three spots, and I had to do a solo spot, with song too. We would
also have a feature called 'New Voices' (with another signature
tune by Harry Pepper); 'Chestnut Corner', old gags presented with
funny noises between each gag; and a sketch about a rag-and-bone
man called 'Mr Walker wants to know' played by that fine comic
actor, Sid Walker. We also decided to have a guest star each week.
And on 5 January (the date is engraved on my heart) we launched
Band Waggon.

THE BBC publicity department now started to get busy with their new brain-child. I was tagged 'The Resident Comedian' and all the national newspapers carried the same story, like this one in the *Daily Mail*:

RADIO CAUSERIE
NOVEL IDEA
— — — — — — —
Comedian's Serial
Programme
———
ARTHUR ASKEY THE
LUCKY MAN
———

An idea, novel in every respect to broadcasting in this country was approved by the B.B.C. Programme Board today.

A comedian has been selected, material will be written round him, and in the New Year he will broadcast every Wednesday night for twelve weeks. Such a contract has never before been given to a radio comedian in this country.

> The programmes will be in serial form to the extent that the same artists and characters will be retained, but each episode will be complete in itself. Each instalment will present a problem which listeners will be asked to assist in solving.
>
> ### Great Opportunity
>
> Arthur Askey is the comedian who receives the new contract and there is little doubt that at the end of the twelve weeks his name should be a household word.
>
> It is an opportunity radio artists dream about, a much-desired continuity which has – with certain rare exceptions – never been attainable.
>
> It is a step nearer the regularising of programmes which makes for easier and more discriminate listening.

As the day of the first broadcast of *Band Waggon* approached, I began to get a bit anxious. At rehearsals it was obvious that the script was not very good, and Dickie and I just could not shake any life into it. Also I was still busy with *The Boy Who Lost His Temper* at the Cambridge Theatre, as well as my usual concert and cabaret appearances, and did not have the time to give the script the attention it sadly required. The features seemed to be all right and the eight-piece orchestra of 'Phil Cardew and his Band Waggoners', with a vocal trio called 'The Jackdaws', was excellent.

As I have mentioned, my mother destroyed any press notices which were in the least anti-Askey. Fortunately, I am therefore unable to quote any of the criticisms we received for the first *Band Waggon*. We were all very depressed about it and we all had long faces when we met for rehearsals for the next show. The second show was not much better: the guest star was the American singer, Harry Richman – the Sinatra of his day – and he took the curse off the comedy. The third show was very mediocre and the only laughs we got were those that Dickie and I had inserted into the script.

After that John Watt, having decided to cancel the series after six programmes, allowed us to do what we liked with the scripts. So with this new freedom Dickie and I started work on the fourth programme. We realised that our efforts would have to be such that they would save the series. One of the new ideas was the Top Flat at the BBC headquarters. I suggested that as I was tagged the Resident Comedian, I should live on the premises and the comedy would be built around this. The BBC top brass did not like the idea – they took themselves very seriously in those days – but I was determined to try and save the ship, or the waggon, and put my foot down. So Dickie, Vernon Harris, Gordon Crier, and myself sat around a table in the smallest office in St George's Hall and churned out the script for *Band Waggon* Number 4. It seemed to come to life and everybody was very much happier. We also had Art Tatum, the fantastic blind American pianist, as the guest, which helped things along. By the time we got to programme Number 6, John Watt had removed his threat to take the show off, and when we reached the contracted twelfth programme he offered us a further series of six programmes. We could not do any more than that as I soon had to rehearse for my summer show at the beginning of May. Rex Newman had made a smart move and booked Dickie Murdoch for the 'Fol-de-Rols' as well.

By the time we had finished twelve *Band Waggons* we were very popular, but at the end of eighteen we were national favourites. Our catchphrases were being used everywhere: 'I thank you' (or 'Aythangyow') being the number one. This I had picked up from the London bus conductors and didn't even realise I was saying it! I called myself 'Big-hearted', and Dickie was christened 'Stinker'. 'Playmates' was the name I coined for the audience as, after the first programme, I received a letter from Tommy Handley telling me off for saying 'Hello, folks' which he claimed was his. I also coined 'Don't be filthy', 'Doesn't it make you want to spit' (I always was a Society entertainer!) 'Light the blue paper and retire immediately', while Dickie consistently called me 'You silly little man'. We decided we would have a charwoman to help us in the flat, and set about finding a name for her. One day in the street we saw a van with the words 'Diploma Bagwash' on the side, and we decided Mrs Bagwash was the name we were looking for. We also decided that she should have a daughter called Diploma. When we told Harry Pepper, he laughed a lot and said the names were perfect. However, when we told him where we had found them he said, 'You can't call the daughter "Diploma", that would be advertising.'

I said, 'Oh, you fill me with nausea,' and then, 'Wait a minute, that's an even better name for her, Nausea Bagwash,' and so the Bagwashes were launched. Neither of them spoke throughout the series: Mrs B. gave an occasional grunt when spoken to, while Nausea always fainted in front of the microphone and all you ever heard was a thud.

We decided we could now do without guest artistes and the last one was Cary Grant. We gave him a script in which he tried to steal Nausea (now my girlfriend) from me. He was bewildered by it, but I said, 'You just read it and you'll get big laughs,' and by golly, he did. He thanked me after the show; in fact he wrote on my script (which I still have) 'Thanks a lot, cock, Cary'.

By this time we had installed Lewis the goat in the flat. This came about when Dickie and I decided it was too far to go down a flight of forty-nine stairs, and then down seven floors in the lift, to get the morning milk. So we bought the goat, the whole point being that we could use the gag: 'A goat in the flat – what about the smell?' 'Oh, he'll get used to it!'

We also had two pigeons, Lucy and Basil. Dickie made a splendid cooing noise, while I gave a 'fluttering' sound by waving my script about. For a time, we introduced Hector the camel, but soon realised that we were overdoing it and being downright silly, so Hector had to go. For hygienic purposes we used the 'Announcers' Bathroom' which was conveniently situated right under our flat and where we could hear Stuart Hibberd singing in the morning. We found our chimney went straight down into the Director General's fireplace where there was always a fire burning. So when we wanted to boil a couple of eggs, we put them in a kettle which we let down on a string on to the fire and sang two choruses of 'Hands, knees and bumps-a-daisy' to ensure that they were hard-boiled before we pulled them up.

The features in *Band Waggon* were all going well. 'Mr Walker wants to know' was a big success and received a big mail in response to Sid Walker's closing line 'What would you do, chums?' 'Chestnut Corner' was very popular with its collection of old gags and some cleverly inserted new ones, and, of course, the funny noises between each joke. 'New Voices' gave a lot of beginners a chance: perhaps the most successful was Ruby Moule, later Vanessa Lee,

Above: 'The Love Racket'.

Right: In 'Follow the Girls', 1945.

Opposite page, Top: A clutch
of comics: Stan Laurel,
Sid Field, Val Parnell,
Danny Kaye, and me.
Opposite page, Bottom:
Rehearsing a Royal Command
Performance.

Top: The Command
Performance that never was:
George (Liberace's brother),
Max Bygraves, Liberace, me
and Jimmy Wheeler, 1956.
Bottom: Meeting her Majesty
the Queen and Prince Philip,
at the Command Performance,
Blackpool, 1955.

Above: Approaching New York.

Left: In New York, with Olsen and Johnson.

the star of Ivor Novello's Drury Lane triumphs. A lovely girl with a lovely voice and a divine sense of comedy.

So great was the compulsive listening to *Band Waggon* that Wednesday night services at churches had to be altered, the Post Office had an enquiry as to why there were less calls between eight and nine on a Wednesday evening, and theatre and cinema business was affected. 'Big' and 'Stinker' had really arrived. When I was announced at my concerts, my reception was noticeably more audible, and the autograph signing – then a novelty for me – became part of a way of life. And they wanted my signature for themselves, not like now when it's always for 'my grandmother', 'my brother', 'my little girl', which always makes my hair bristle.

We finished the eighteenth edition of *Band Waggon* with the promise that we would be returning in the autumn. The BBC was receiving hundreds of letters complaining because the show was being taken off, so we had to tell the listeners that we'd be back. Dickie and I commenced rehearsals for the 'Fol-de-Rols' at the Goat and Compasses pub in Euston Road and found ourselves in the company of Jack Warner (Evening, all!!), Walter Midgley (later principal tenor at Covent Garden), and Gladys Merredew, the comedienne who had been with me at Shanklin for six years and who had left to join the 'Fol-de-Rols' at Hastings the previous season. You may remember that I told you earlier that my reason for giving Shanklin a rest was my difficulty in finding new material each season. Imagine my delight when Gladys told me, very shame-facedly, that she had already done most of my repertoire, including 'The Bee'. I complained to my new guv'nor but he told me not to worry as nobody could sing my songs like I could! Who was I to argue!

We broke the show in at Torquay for two weeks where the business was fantastic. The 'Fol-de-Rols' were always great favourites at Torquay, and there was now the added attraction of 'Big' and 'Stinker'. We moved on to Hastings for an eighteen-week season and here again we proved our popularity with capacity business the whole time.

My little missus had rented a flat for us on the Marine Parade, with a beautiful outlook over the sea, but, oh! the stairs. At least in our top flat at Broadcasting House we had a lift. I cannot remember how many stairs we had to climb (with Anthea only five

years of age), but once we started downstairs, I made certain I
didn't have to go back for anything. Our landlord was Colonel
Tubbs, who lived on the premises, and had a very ancient man-
servant who brought up our meals from the basement. The tray
and all the dishes were solid silver and the poor fellow had to carry
the lot up six flights to our flat. We would hear him arrive and
listen to his heavy breathing before he could raise the strength to
knock at the door. The first day, the Colonel had sent up a dozen
oysters for me in addition to the normal meal. As the poor chap
staggered in with the load he gasped, referring to the oysters, 'With
Colonel Tubbs' compliments,' tripped on the carpet and promptly
dropped the lot. I almost booked him for the show!

We had a very happy show at the White Rock Pavilion, and the
company could not have been nicer, or more talented. Jack Warner
was marvellous with his Maurice Chevalier impressions, and Dickie
and I could do no wrong, but the real hit of the programme was
Walter Midgley whose superb singing stopped the show every night.
My parents and sister came down for their holidays and with my
May and Anthea we spent every day on the beach. Dickie's wife,
Peggy Rawlings, was the soubrette in the show, so everything was
cosy and friendly. The only cloud on the horizon was the threat of
war with Germany. However, Mr Chamberlain came back waving
his bit of paper and assuring us that there was to be 'peace in our
time', so with this security Dickie and I started to discuss new ideas
for the forthcoming series of *Band Waggon*.

We had a wonderfully warm reception back on the air and everybody, including the critics, said 'better than ever'. I was asked to
make my first record (of 'The Bee', naturally) and I was approached
by Gaumont British to make a film, an offer which eventually
turned into a contract for eight pictures, with options. I went to
Horace Reeves, the agent who had earlier approached me to play
the Music Halls. Within two days, he rang me and said that the
Stoll circuit had offered me seventy-five pounds a week at Shepherds
Bush Empire and Hackney Empire to share the top of the bill with
Mollie Picon, the American comedienne. I dug my heels in and
still insisted on one hundred pounds and top of the bill. And I won.
Now I started to worry. I had always been scared of playing the
Halls, for I never felt I was 'broad' enough. I was still essentially

concert party in my approach and I had seen some popular radio artistes who had 'died' on the Halls. I remember Mabel Constanduros at the Alhambra, with Joe Beckett – then the reigning heavyweight champion – topping the bill with a boxing exhibition. The audience consisted of men with broken noses and cauliflower ears and you can imagine how interested they were in Mabel's chat about 'Gran'ma'! Leonard Henry had a struggle on the same bill, as did most of the radio/concert party comedians at the various Music Halls. Was it to be my turn now?

When I turned up for Monday morning rehearsal at Shepherds Bush, the stage manager asked me how long I was going to do. I said, 'It depends on how I go!' He said, 'What do you mean?' I said, 'If I'm going well, I'll do about twenty minutes; if they don't like me, I'll be off like a startled ferret.' He said, 'Oh you can't do that on the Halls – you've got to keep to a time.' Seeing my bewilderment, he said, 'Look, I'll put you down for twelve minutes, okay?' I gulped 'Okay' and prepared myself for the worst. The manager came around and said, 'We are booked out solid for the week – it has never happened before.' This made me more nervous than ever, so I decided I would do my full twenty-minute concert act in the space of the allotted twelve minutes. I thought, 'If I go very fast, they won't have a chance to "get" at me!' And that's what I did – how, I shall never know. There has never been a quicker act in the history of show biz! But I need not have worried. The audiences were *Band Waggon* fans; many had never been in a Music Hall in their lives, and I could do no wrong. By the Wednesday I was getting really cheeky and going well over my allotted twelve minutes. And the stage manager let me know the discipline of the theatre, and told me well off: 'Stick to your time – star or not!'

The following week, I played the Hackney Empire with much more confidence and stuck to my allotted time. Business again was capacity, and this was at a time when Music Halls were in the doldrums. I found that the powers-that-be were taking me off the Stoll tour and putting me on the Moss Empire's circuit – much bigger and more powerful. So the following week I found myself at the Holborn Empire, the variety theatre where I had seen so many of the Music Hall 'greats'. When I had sat in front, I had always noticed the musical director, Syd Kaplan. I had heard such tales about him – how he had bullied artistes into getting new band-parts ('You can't expect my orchestra to play from these dog-eared pieces of manuscript'), which he would score himself, and then further persuaded them to buy new band-books with their names on the front embossed in gold, which cost a pretty penny. It was quite a good sideline for him.

Syd Kaplan made no attempt to sell me a new set of parts – I had only had them a fortnight, so they were in a reasonable state (though the musicians had a habit of putting cryptic signs on them as well as the names of horses, girlfriends, and rude drawings). Syd came into my dressing room, told me how good I was, then said 'Where did you get that dress suit?' Smugly I told him, but he shook his head and said, 'It's very provincial, not nearly good enough for a star artiste of your calibre. Now, I've got a marvellous tailor and I think I could persuade him to make you a lovely pair of tails. I'll ring him in the morning.' Sure enough, the next night, he had fixed an appointment for me in Albemarle Street. I went along and a few days later emerged with a new evening dress suit, dinner jacket, two lounge suits, and a camel-hair overcoat! I can only guess at Syd's commission on this order.

About this time, I was told that Jack Hylton had bought the stage rights of *Band Waggon* and a meeting was arranged between us at my agent's office. I was thrilled to meet Jack, whose band I had always admired. I found him a fascinating character and we struck up a friendship that lasted over twenty-five years. He was a real extrovert and his motto was 'If you think champagne, you'll drink champagne.' He had a house in Oxfordshire, a house at Angmering, a house just off Grosvenor Square, a flat at Marble Arch, and a house at Antibes in the south of France. He had several cars, several horses, and assorted mistresses. He lived like Nero of old and was, naturally, a good Socialist! During my years with him, he made far more money out of Arthur Askey than I did. It started at our first meeting. Without me, *Band Waggon* meant nothing and I could have demanded anything when we began to talk money. To be fair, he asked me if I would like to take a percentage instead of a salary. My agent asked to be excused, took me into another room, and said, 'Don't fall for that – he's a sharp practitioner. You take a salary and be on the safe side.' Whether this was connivance, I shall never know. My agent lived on the same estate as Jack Hylton at Angmering, and I have an idea the carving up of the little concert party comic took place at the golf club down there at weekends.

Anyway, I signed to do the stage show of *Band Waggon* which was to be produced in the early spring of 1939. Meanwhile, the radio show was going on from strength to strength on Wednesday nights. I was beginning to meet and hob-nob with celebrities and I had my life-story serialised in *Tit-Bits*, a humorous column (ghosted) in *The Sunday Chronicle*, and *The Arthur Askey Annual* lined up for publication at Christmas by the Oxford University Press. There was only one edition of this; it was killed off by the war. I appeared in a comic strip on the front page of *Radio Fun*, there were Askey dolls and glove puppets, and badges sold at Woolworth's. In one of our *Band Waggon* episodes, Dickie and I concocted a mixture, intended to make rock-cakes, that finished up as a cleansing powder. We called it 'Askitoff' and coined the slogan 'Askitoff will take it off'. We pretended we were going to sell it behind the BBC's back and kept plugging it all the time. I received two or three enquiries from the large industrial companies of the day, asking if they could use the title and 'how much?' I wrote and said, 'Wait until we finish the series and we'll be able to talk business. Meanwhile, we'll keep plugging it.' We arrived to do our weekly broadcast one Wednesday and Harry Pepper said, 'Sorry, boys, but you must not mention Askitoff again.' Two fellows had registered the title and there was nothing we could do about it. It came on to the market as 'Askitoff – Britain's Best Cleanser' (BBC) and had a big heart (my trademark) on the label. The American magazine *Life* did a two-page spread on the story: they were intrigued, as all American radio programmes were commercially sponsored and it amused them to see the BBC clamping down in the way it did.

Then there were the amazing gifts we received. In addition to hundreds of pairs of 'combs' (combinations) which came my way – I was always talking about 'me combs' – I had only to mention any article on the air and it would be sent to me. For instance, Dickie and I were cutting out a shirt with the aid of a pattern book that stated the edges wanted 'pinking'. So we got a bottle of red ink, which I promptly upset over the material. I said, 'Do you

know, Stinker – I've always wanted a pink shirt.' The following
week I had dozens sent to me, so I thanked the listeners and said,
'I wish I'd said I wanted a bottle of Scotch.' Sure enough, dozens
of bottles of Scotch – chiefly miniatures, I'm sorry to say – began
to arrive. I acknowledged these the week after and said, 'I've tried
to force a grand piano into the script this week.' Believe it or not, I
must have received a hundred pianos, from tiny ones containing a
bottle of perfume to two-octave practical toy pianos. I once did a
recitation entitled 'Picture if you can, a winkle'. A few days later a
large wooden crate was delivered at my flat and my wife and I
could not make out what it could be. We dragged it into the kitchen,
and I got a hammer and a screwdriver and attacked it. All of a
sudden, it collapsed and out fell thousands of winkles. We were
ankle-deep in them!

So in autumn 1938 this was my life: playing all the London
Music Halls – often two a night – and fitting in the hour's broadcast on the Wednesday as well. In addition, I was doing the odd
cabaret or concert, and certainly appeared somewhere or other
every Sunday. I now had a new American car, a Hudson, and a
chauffeur, as well as a pianist.

The whole country now knew Arthur Askey. I was playing Fins-
bury Park Empire when the stage-door keeper said Mr Arthur
Greenwood, a Cabinet minister at that time, wanted to see me. He
came into my dressing room and said, 'I feel I must meet you as all
my constituents call me "Big-hearted Arthur".' He then told me
he and the rest of the Cabinet had been at a meeting with the
King and the King had laughed his head off, telling them all the
funny things I had said and done in *Band Waggon* the previous
evening. Arthur Greenwood said, 'Either he is not a very good
raconteur, or you're not very funny!' But when he left, I rushed to
the phone to tell my wife and my mother: 'What do you know –
the King listens to me!'

I only ever went home to sleep. My daughter Anthea to this day
calls me 'Wave'. When she was little, which, by the way, she still is,
May would bring her to the front door as I was driving off and
say, 'Wave'. I came home one night and said to Anthea, 'Hello,
darling,' and she said, 'Hello, Wave,' and the name has stuck ever
since.

As all the Music Halls in and around London were preparing for their annual pantomimes, it looked as if I was going to take things a little easier over the Christmas of 1938. But I had reckoned without Jack Hylton. At the last minute, he decided he would bring forward the proposed stage version of *Band Waggon* and produce it at the Princes Theatre (now the Shaftesbury) which was unoccupied, as it was most of the year in those days. We opened at the Princes on Boxing Day and, together with Jack Hylton's Band, we had in the show some strong variety acts, including 'Afrique' the impressionist (very popular at that time for his impersonation of the Prince of Wales). Dickie Murdoch, Syd Walker, and all the *Band Waggon* features were of course included. The Press notices were far from favourable – the only one to come out of it with any credit was a youngster who appeared in the feature 'New Voices'. He was a fresh-faced good-looking lad from Leeds who appeared in evening dress (with clogs!) and sang and tap-danced with all the assurance of a fourteen-year-old. His name was Ernie Wise. Jack Hylton prophesied a big future for him, as he also did for Eric Morecambe the following year, and I thought he was joking! Sorry, Eric and Ernie!

Despite an apparently strong show, business was lousy, and we ran for only three of the four weeks booked at the Princes. I was bitterly disappointed. In the week before Christmas (a week notorious for failure in show business) I had appeared by myself just 500 yards away at the Holborn Empire and had played to capacity audiences. Lack of publicity was the main reason for this disaster.

The show was represented in early 1939 at the Gaumont, Holloway, and this time, with proper backing and publicity, we filled the three-thousand-seater three times a day. And for the next few weeks we did similar business at all the Music Halls and large cinemas that we played. Dickie Murdoch developed appendicitis and had to leave the show for a month, but we found an excellent deputy in a charming, good-looking chap called Peter Vokes who, early in the war, was promoted to lieutenant and, sadly, killed in 1940. Dickie resumed and we continued our usual routines, but our *Band Waggon* radio broadcasts were drawing to a close. The BBC was desperately keen to keep it on, but Hylton knew he had a money-spinner on his hands, especially, as, released from this commitment, we would be able to go into the provinces. The papers were full of protests from both the critics and the public, but business is business. I said it was a relief, the strain of finding new material every week was beginning to tell, and I would have hated our high standard to have dropped.

So it was with tears all round that we did our last *Band Waggon* after about fifty programmes in all. When you consider that *ITMA*, *Take it from Here*, *Much Binding* etc., each went on for at least ten years, our show seemed to have a very short run indeed, but I flatter myself to think that we made the biggest impact. The number of people who remember the show with great affection, even after a lapse of thirty-five years, regularly surprises me. (And I don't mean that I'm still receiving pairs of long combs!)

Anyway, we were now preparing to tour the provinces. Jack Hylton, shrewdly thinking that he could double his money, sent Syd Walker out separately with 'Mr Walker wants to know', while we included a version of it, played by that great 'Fred Karno' comedian, Fred Kitchen. We were to open at the Hippodrome,

Birmingham, not for one week, but three! The bookings were fantastic. The *Birmingham Mail* said the management had been:

> inundated with letters, phone calls, cheques, postal orders, cajoling and imploring them to let the writers or callers have seats. Before the booking office actually opened, the ever-growing crowd had extended the whole length of Inge Street, along Essex Street and around the corner into Horse Fair, and later it extended around the thoroughfare and down Thorp Street, until the tail-end came in view of the front portion entering the booking-office.

David Cassidy, Donny Osmond, and the like – please note!

I was asked what time I was arriving in Birmingham on the Sunday as they wanted to have a band meet me at the station. I said I couldn't give them a time and in any event, I would be travelling by road. I had booked in at the Midland Hotel and been given the Chamberlain Suite – much too big for May and me, but I felt I had to put on a display now that I was a 'great star'! We arrived at the hotel and had started to unpack when the band struck up outside our window and serenaded us. We were too frightened to even peep through the curtains. We later went down for dinner and in order to be unobtrusive I asked the head waiter for a table near the door. A gentleman diner who had obviously had too much to drink swayed towards the exit, caught sight of me, and shouted to his friend who was still sitting at their table, 'Look who's here. Two funny jokes and "The Bee" song – fifty thousand a year.' You can imagine how May and I felt, with all the dining room customers staring at us. But it was a taste of things to come – incidents I hated, which distressed my little wife immeasurably.

We opened at the Hippodrome and were a tremendous success, thanks to our radio reputations. I doubt if we would have gone as well if we had been unknown. Jimmy Wheeler and his father (Wheeler & Wilson) were on the bill, as were the Henderson Twins and Sonny (Sonny being my great mate in later years) Dickie Henderson.

I found that my great hero Leslie Henson was playing at the Prince of Wales Theatre in *Going Greek*, and although I had seen the show in London, I immediately booked to see the star again at the Wednesday matinée. I had just taken my seat in the circle, when an attendant brought me a note which read 'Mr Leslie Henson would be delighted to meet Mr Arthur Askey in his dressing room after the performance.' I was so excited at the prospect of at last meeting my idol that I could hardly watch the show. I rushed around at the finish and was ushered into the great Leslie's dressing room. I almost knelt down in his presence and babbled, 'Oh, Mr Henson – I can't tell you how pleased I am to meet you.' Leslie rolled his eyes and said in that marvellous croaky voice of his, 'Well, I'm not very pleased to see you – you've ruined our bloody business this week!'

So our triumphant *Band Waggon* tour went on – everywhere the same – two or three weeks' stay in a major city, each one booked out on our arrival—even in Glasgow, where English comics were normally frightened to appear (Des O'Connor tells how he fainted on the stage there). Prior to visiting Glasgow, I had been receiving letters in my enormous mail telling me that when I got there I would be 'done' by a gang called the Billy Boys. The letters were filthy and abusive, but I imagined that they were from some cranks who had nothing better to do. By chance I showed these to a police inspector who called at my dressing room at Streatham Hill Theatre one evening – probably asking me to appear at a police concert, which I was always happy to do. He phoned me a few days later and said they were taking the matter seriously and I would have police protection when I arrived in Glasgow.

For the first time on the tour I had booked 'digs' instead of a hotel. They had been highly recommended by George Robey, but when I arrived there, they were in a kind of tenement block in a not very salubrious neighbourhood. We opened at the Empire with a two-week booking and were so successful that we stayed for an additional week. But every night when I left the theatre, there were two policemen at the stage door and they hustled me through the crowds (of my adoring fans!) into my car, and I was whisked away. Nothing happened until the last day I was there, when I received a letter saying 'Tonight's the night,' and signed 'The Billy Boys'. I contacted the Chief Constable who said he would have a couple of extra men on duty that evening, which made me feel better. I'm no hero! During the evening, I had several callers and had run out of Scotch, so I sent my pianist out for a bottle. He came back, white-faced, and said he had been in the pub next door and there had been a fight, with broken bottles as weapons, between two gangs in the pub. And one of the gangs was – you've guessed. Perhaps the fight took the steam out of them because nothing further happened to me, but it was an incident that made me think that perhaps I would have been better staying in London and doing my Masonics.

The tour continued with visits to Edinburgh, Manchester, Coventry, and then Liverpool. I had rather dreaded this, as I knew I would be inundated with relatives and friends, and the 'in-betweens' you always have to pretend you remember. At the same time, deep inside me I felt exhilarated by the thought that I was a local boy who had made good.

Dickie Murdoch and I were at this period doing a weekly series for Radio Luxembourg, which had moved in very quickly when we finished at the BBC. We did a *Band Waggon* type show, and our singer was Al Bowlly, a real heart-throb in those days. Tragically, he was killed in the bombing later. As part of our contract, we had to appear in a major store which sold Symington's products in every town we visited. So when we arrived in Liverpool, we were advertised to do our stint at Coopers in Church Street. The streets around the store were alive with people, while inside they were crammed to the doors. With a police escort, Dickie and I were smuggled in through a back door and taken up to the fourth floor in a lift that was usually used to carry sacks of flour. We appeared to cheers and rounds of applause and, as usual, climbed on to the counter where hundreds of tins of Symington's soups were piled up in pyramids six feet high. The adoring throng kept up the cheers and applause until eventually I quelled the mob and took a deep breath to deliver my blessing, when a bowler hat (that was all I could see of him) in the second row shouted 'When are you coming to see your Aunty Cis?' It was my Uncle Charlie who had obviously been celebrating his nephew's success. Dickie Murdoch laughed so much that he knocked over all the tins and then fell off the counter backwards.

So much for my first visit as a star to my native city, for which

I naturally have a great affection. There is a huge statue of a naked man outside Lewis's store in the centre of Liverpool, and whenever I appear at the Empire, I always say how touched I am that they put up that 'wonderful statue of me, outside Lewis's'. I then add, 'Perhaps you didn't realise it was me, as when I posed for it, I took off my glasses – or didn't you look at the face.' The most prominent feature of the statue is very obvious when it rains, as the water runs off the end, most realistically!!

Our tour was now ending and we were told we were booked at the London Palladium for the summer. Naturally we were all very excited because apart from being the most important variety theatre in the world, it meant we could all live at home. Touring can become a chore when it goes on too long. George Black, the impresario who 'made' the Palladium, always had difficulty with the summer months. The Crazy Gang filled the theatre to capacity all winter, but the three or four months between their shows were, for him, a headache. *Band Waggon* solved his problem – you would have thought from the business we did that The Crazy Gang had never left. We were supported by other big names and I was more than delighted to find my old Shanklin rival Tommy Trinder on the bill, also Jack Durrant, the American comedian, and a fantastic American act called Wild Willy West and McGinty. We opened on 3 July 1939 to a tremendous reception and we knew the business was going to be capacity for the run. I remember being on stage with Tommy on several occasions and spotting Bud and Ches, Nervo and Knox, and Naughton and Gold standing at the back of the stalls watching us and Tommy shouting, 'How about this – two men doing the work of six!'

We had a very happy show at the Palladium. Tommy was really great fun. Jack Durrant was, as I have said, a very 'with-it' American who looked like Clark Gable. The big gimmick in his act was a marvellous 'back-flip' he used to do. He would say, 'Clark Gable – a great actor, but can he do this?' and do his acrobatic back-somersault. Then, 'Arthur Askey – a funny little man, but can he do this?' and repeat the trick. He said to Tommy, 'They have booked me at the Holborn Empire (he pronounced it 'Hole-bourne') and I have got to go there as soon as I have finished my act here. Who can I talk about on the bill there?' Tommy thought quickly and said, 'Caryll and Mundy are topping the bill: just say "Billy Caryll – can he do this?" and you'll get a big laugh.' As soon as Durrant had left for the Holborn, Tommy got on the phone to Billy Caryll and tipped him off. Now Billy was a very good acrobat, so when Jack said, 'Billy Caryll – a very good comedian, but can he do this?' Billy stepped from the wings and said, 'Of course I can,' and did it, saying as he exited, 'But I don't have to!'

Tommy was appearing at the Coconut Grove night-club as well as the Palladium and he told me one evening that they were expecting a visit from Orson Welles that night. So I went along hoping to see the great man – he really was a super-star in those days. Midnight arrived, but Orson hadn't, so Tommy started his act to 'You lucky people'. He'd been going for about five minutes when Orson arrived with his party, so Tommy started his ad libbing 'Had trouble with the bike,' etc. When Welles and his party eventually sat down, Tommy welcomed him and said his usual 'Trinder's the name' and Orson Welles snapped back, 'Why don't you change it?' Tommy, quick as a flash, said, 'Are you proposing?'

While at the Palladium, I signed my contract with Gainsborough Films and agreed to commence shooting in late August. I couldn't wait, although I knew it meant working all day, with two performances to cope with at the Palladium at night. In addition, the show was going so well they had put on extra matinées on Wednesday and Saturday. But I was young and healthy and a glutton for work. (Even now, when I'm old and reasonably healthy, I'm still a glutton for work.) Everything was going my way and the only cloud on the horizon was another comedian called Adolf Hitler who I had an uneasy feeling was going to spoil things for me and everybody else.

I started shooting my first film during the last week in August. Naturally it was called *Band Waggon* and was supposed to be the story of what happened to Dickie and me when we left our flat at the end of our stint for the BBC. It started with the lift in Broadcasting House opening its doors on the ground floor, to disclose Dickie and me perched on top of a heap of decrepit furniture and trying to disentangle ourselves and get out. Mr Middleton, who was then the BBC's Percy Thrower (he did the gardening talks), happened to be passing and we said, 'Oh, Mr Middleton, will you

help us? We want to get out of here. How should we go about it?'
and he replied, 'Well, to start with, I should cut away all that dead
wood,' etc. The film was to be made at the Gainsborough studios
at Islington and we were told to report at eight o'clock on the morning of Monday, 29 August. I had been given a script beforehand,
so had dutifully learned the first half a dozen pages. Nobody had
told me that you never start a film at the beginning – I had to learn
such things as I went along. The director was an excitable French-
man called Marcel Varnel. He had directed the Crazy Gang pictures and his great asset was his speed. He was paid a bonus which
depended on how quickly he finished a film. His big catchphrase
was 'Vy are ve vaiting?' He used to sit under the camera waving his
handkerchief during every shot, and when he was satisfied he always said, 'Cut – print – give me a view-finder – oooh, Christ!'
This was when he banged his head on the camera as he sprang up
from his chair.

I enjoyed my first week as a film star (?) and the rush to the
Palladium when we'd finished shooting. I hardly had time to read
the papers or listen to the radio news, and after a hectic week was
glad to relax in my flat on the Sunday morning, that is until I heard
Chamberlain's speech at 11 a.m. announcing that we were now 'at
war with Germany'. A few minutes later there was an air-raid
warning. I was looking through the window and saw an air-raid
warden walking down Golders Green Road when the warning (a
false one, incidentally) went. He managed to blow his whistle and
promptly fainted on the pavement.

May and Anthea had just returned the previous day from two
weeks' holiday at Worthing, so I bundled them into the car and took
them back again. The radio informed us that all theatres, cinemas,
and studios were to close, so I stayed down in Worthing with the
family, reflecting on what would happen to my career. After fifteen
years' struggle to get my name in lights, came the black-out! To
say I was depressed is to put it mildly. However, after about three
weeks, I was informed that I was required at the studios. They were
going to recommence filming, this time at Lime Grove Studios,
Shepherds Bush. I couldn't wait to get there and pick up where we
had left off. Well, not exactly. Quite a few of the artistes and the
crew had been called up, so we had to re-shoot several items.

Jack Hylton (with his band) was in the film and he told me there was a furnished house to let near his own, at Rustington, Sussex, and why, if I wanted to keep my family out of London, didn't I rent it and spend the weekends down there? This I did, and for a couple of years I did what the rich people do – had a flat in town and a house in the country. Jack had taken little Ernie Wise to stay with him and I can still see Ernie on his bike coming into our kitchen and asking my wife if she wanted anything from the shops. He was always cycling, which must be responsible for the 'short – fat – hairy legs'!

With the threat of air-raids, I brought my mother, father, and sister to Sussex, so we had all the Askey Clan under one roof. Jack Hylton was commuting between Rustington and the studios, so I joined him in his chauffeur-driven Rolls each day. He collected me at six in the morning and during the journey he used to tell me fascinating stories of his travels with his band, all over Europe (including Russia) and America, as well as in this country. The only drawback was that he smoked his first cigar of the day while he was talking, and at six in the morning, I must admit to feeling very queasy by the time we arrived at Lime Grove. We used to leave the studios about six in the evening to drive back, and on the journey he would stop the car at the butcher's or confectioner's and buy a couple of meat pies, which he loved. It must have been his Lancashire blood. He would then go into a sweet shop and buy a pound of liquorice all-sorts and nibble all the way home, with a cigar going at the same time! It was during this period that Jack gave me a very useful tip. I had started to receive a huge fan mail and amongst the usually eulogistic letters there were the occasional stinkers. These would be mostly anonymous and invariably told me in strong words to 'give up', or that I 'deserved shooting', etc. Naturally I felt rather indignant at receiving such letters and whenever they arrived with a signature and address attached, I was inclined to write a suitable reply. Jack, however, advised me to reply along the lines of 'Thank you for your nice letter. I enclose herewith a signed photograph as requested.' This usually worked: often I would receive either an apology or a retraction of the correspondent's accusation. Sometimes, however, the photograph was returned with interesting additions scrawled on my lovely features!

Perhaps Jack Hylton's shrewdness was due to the fact that his most frequent companions were politicians, and always of the Labour Party. It was fortunate, however, that Jack got cold feet and withdrew his nomination after offering himself as Labour candidate for Bolton. After all, he was no orator, and in fact his only effective speech was 'Ah-one-two-three' when leading his band into their numbers. Jack never received the knighthood that he wanted so badly, although Lord Goodman once told me that Jack would have done so had he lived two or three months longer. (He died in 1965.) At least he received one worthy decoration – that of the Legion of Honour, presented to him by the President of France in the mid-thirties. What a character Jack was – they don't breed them like him any more.

The film seemed to be going very well and we were keeping up to schedule, thanks to the drive of director Marcel Varnel. I did a scene where I sang one of my 'bird' songs, and had to fly over the band on a wire as I warbled away, flailing my arms about. I was put into my flying harness first thing in the morning and as I was attired in full evening dress, I was not feeling too happy as the morning wore on. Flying harnesses are not the most comfortable things to wear under your clothes, especially for the male!! It was getting near lunchtime and I still hadn't done the scene, so I said I was going to take the harness off. Marcel insisted that I kept the wretched thing on saying, 'Ve do a rehearsal before lunch, then film it first thing thees afternoon.' I must admit I grumbled quite a bit; however, I was hauled up despite my protests. I was hoisted up and up until I was right up against the ceiling, and as you know, a film studio is a pretty lofty place. As I touched the ceiling, Marcel shouted, 'Okay, break for lunch. Back at two o'clock,' and the entire studio emptied. I never felt more lonely or impotent in my life. There was nothing I could do but 'hang around'. After what seemed a lifetime (actually about three minutes) they came back and let me down. I felt very sore about it – in more ways than one – and resolved never to grumble again on a film set.

The BBC approached Dickie and me about doing another series of *Band Waggon*, which we needed like a hole in the head. But we were told the request had come from very high up and, when we agreed to do it, we were very flattered to hear Sir John Simon say

in the House of Commons, 'We are getting back to normality –
Band Waggon will be back on the air next week.' This is recorded
in Hansard. The BBC had moved to Bristol by this time, so to do
the broadcasts Dickie and I had to travel down there on Friday
nights after each week's filming, broadcast the show on Saturday
nights, then get back to Lime Grove to recommence filming at
eight o'clock on Sunday mornings. We used to start writing the
scripts on the train from Paddington to Bristol, and carry on writing
in the hotel until such time as we had finished the job, often at four
in the morning. We did another ten programmes in all – don't ask
me how we managed it, but I think we kept up the high standard.
I remember that in the first one we 'blacked out' the flat in com-
pliance with the regulations. We didn't have any black-out material,
so we covered the window with Pontefract cakes, only to find when
we switched on the light that we had covered the overmantel instead.

Theatres were now reopening and I had an urgent call from my
agent asking me if I would do pantomime for Emile Littler at the
Prince of Wales Theatre, Birmingham. The salary offered was £150
a week, and 'Mr Littler must know by tomorrow'. I couldn't understand the urgency and thought that I was worth at least £500 a
week, but my agent, whom I christened 'I-advise-you-to-take-it-
Reeves', pointed out the uncertainty of everything. He said it was
'a bird in hand' situation, so once again I signed knowing full well
I had been undersold yet again.

We finished filming *Band Waggon* and I was told the option had
been taken up and I was to report for my next picture, *Charlie's
'Big-hearted' Aunt*, in two weeks' time. So Jack Hylton got busy
and booked the Colston Hall, Bristol, for the stage show of *Band
Waggon* to fill the two weeks in question. I secretly could have done
with a rest, but would not admit to being tired – I'm still the same
today.

One night in the hotel, Jack asked me if he could see my film
contract. After he'd read it, he said, 'You've got them over a barrel,
they didn't send you a registered letter saying they were taking up
the option.' I said, 'Oh, it doesn't matter, I want to make the film
in any case,' but Jack was made of sterner stuff. He sent the Gainsborough tycoons a telegram saying I was not going to make the
film. So down to Bristol came the producers, directors, solicitors,

lawyers – all the movie Mafia – and foregathered at the Grand Hotel. Jack Hylton said, 'Go and see them, Arthur, and send for me when you want me!' Needless to say, I soon did want him. I was told that all the cast had been booked – Felix Aylmer, Jeanne de Casalis, Phyllis Calvert, Moore Marriot, Graham Moffat among others, that the studios had been made available, with all the production staff, and that if I did not fulfil my contract, they would take me to court – all kinds of dire threats. Jack (and his solicitor) just said, 'You did not send Arthur a registered letter taking up the option, so you haven't a leg to stand on.' After hours of bargaining, they agreed to double my original fee. Then the true Jack came out. He said, 'Well, I've got you an extra £2,500 for the film – I think it is only fair you should pay me half of what you've gained.' So he made £1,250 out of the deal. Personally I would have been quite happy to have not caused any trouble at all and made the picture for the £2,500 originally contracted. But that's the story of my life: I am quite happy to be working, causing no trouble to impresarios, managers, agents, or producers. I think it pays in the long run. I could name quite a number of well-known and talented performers who were awkward in their heyday, and they have now disappeared into oblivion. As I used to say in *Band Waggon*, 'It isn't the people who make the most noise who do the most work!'

The script of the new film was basically the old farce especially tailored for me, hence the *Charley's 'Big-hearted' Aunt*, and very good it was too. I saw it recently on television and it stood up very well to the test of time. Jack Benny made a film of *Charley's Aunt* about the same time, and I naturally went to see it. As I entered the cinema, the manager said, 'It's not a patch on yours, Arthur,' and, Benny-admirer that I am, I came out agreeing with what the man said.

We used the studio tank for the scene in which I was supposed to fall into the river – dressed as a woman, of course. I was to be rescued by a very statuesque girl – a swimming champion – and as the scene had to be shot several times, we both had changing booths on the set, to get out of our wet clothes and into dry ones. There were no roofs on the cubicle, and the young lady stripped off, unconscious of the fact that all the male staff were up on the gantry enjoying the view! I hadn't the time! I had a scene with Jeanne de

Casalis ('Mrs Feather') where we took tea together with me as a woman. I picked up the tea-pot to pour out and put it down very sharply as the handle was very hot. Jeanne said, 'Why don't you use this?' handing me a round handle-holder. I replied 'Silly me – I thought it was a crumpet!' Perhaps it doesn't sound very funny, but it creased us and we tried take after take but broke down each time we came to the line. The director, Walter Forde, laughed with us at first, then began to get angry. Anyway, we had to postpone shooting the scene until the following day, when we just about managed it. One of those silly things that happen in film-making.

I finished the film just in time to pack a clean shirt and take myself off to Birmingham to rehearse the pantomime. The subject was *Jack and Jill* with a very good 'book' written by Emile himself. I played 'Big-hearted Arthur' – a sort of Buttons part – and found myself in the company of Billy Bennett and the O'Gorman Brothers. I had been warned to expect trouble from them. They were of the old school and people thought they would not be very helpful to a BBC upstart who had top billing. Nothing could have been further from the truth and we made a wonderful team. The O'Gormans involved me in their cod ballet in which they normally used a stooge, and let me do what I liked. And Billy 'Almost a gentleman' Bennett was marvellous. In the schoolroom scene he was 'Professor Twist' and had to ask us 'school-kids' the usual corny pantomime questions. These he had written down in a big book, and many times I hid the book, or altered the lines, and Billy would be absolutely stumped, especially at matinées when he had had a few Pimm's Number Ones at lunchtime. I would sit on the end of my (tip-up) form and say innocently, 'Aren't you going to ask us any questions, teacher?' It was a good job the children couldn't hear what he said to me under his breath! Emile's wife, Cora Griffin, was the principal boy (and a great one at that) and at rehearsals we asked her whose side she was on – the artistes' or the management's. She was with us one hundred per cent, not that we had any trouble with Emile. If he had to tell one of the comics anything about a doubtful gag or time-wasting, he would send him a letter, and send duplicates of the letter to all the other comedians to keep us in the picture. However, he soon stopped it. When we used to spot him at the back of the stalls or in the wings, we would stop whatever we were doing, rush forward and say, 'Any letters?' He enjoyed the joke as much as we did, as well he might, for the business was fantastic and we ran until the middle of April. I was off the show for a week with near-pneumonia. It broke my heart when I read the letters I received from people who had come from great distances, in bad weather (it was a hard winter), to find that I was 'indisposed'.

The pantomime finished on 20 April (an eighteen-week run) and on 21 April I flew to France with Jack Hylton and Dickie Murdoch to entertain the troops, who were having such a boring time during the phoney war period. We landed at Orly airport, went straight to Lens where I did a quick appearance, then on to Arras where I met Gracie Fields for the first time. She had been in France for some two or three weeks and although she was far from well, she worked like the great trouper she always was. I was thrilled to meet her and you can well imagine the reception we got from the troops – Gracie, Jack Hylton and his Band, and Dickie and myself. It was like a Palladium bill, and the lads loved it. We went all over northern France, eventually arriving at Douvai, where the show was broadcast by the BBC to Great Britain. Dickie and I did our 'Proposal' (to Nausea) sketch and H.M.V. record company recorded it and put it out on sale. It reached Number One in the charts.

After a really hectic time, dashing from one town to another, performing in theatres, canteens, even in the open air, we moved on to Paris where we were to give a big show at the Opera House, with Monsieur le President in attendance. I shared a car with Gracie and we arrived at the Ritz (where we were slumming it at the expense of the British Government) at about two in the morning. We were both handed a note and found it was from Maurice Chevalier. Would we meet him in the American bar at twelve o'clock the following day and he would be honoured to take us out to lunch. Gracie was like a schoolgirl: she had never met Maurice and was thrilled at the prospect.

When we met Maurice at midday he kissed Gracie's hand and she did a cod swoon, but I'm certain Maurice was just as thrilled to meet her. He was all charm, and after a cocktail suggested we move off to go to the restaurant where we were to have lunch. There was quite a party, including Jack and Dickie, so when we got outside there was the usual sorting out as to who was to go with whom, and in which car. Maurice had a tiny Citroën (to save petrol, he explained) and said as I was small, I had better go with him. He had a young lady with him and she was doing the driving, so Maurice said, 'I will go in the back and you sit in front with my friend.' I said that was silly and that, as I was titch, I would sit in the back. It was a tinier car than I thought; even I couldn't sit upright in the back! As we drove through Paris, Maurice – the perfect host – was pointing out all the places of interest to me. 'Arthur, there is the Louvre, there is the Opera House, there is la Place de la Concorde,' etc. Eventually he said, 'Arthur, there is Notre-Dame,' and I said, 'I know and I feel like the bloody hunch-back at the back here.' Every time I met Maurice afterwards, he would always greet me by saying, 'How is my little hunch-back?' It really amused him.

We did the big show at l'Opéra the following day. I thought I would air a bit of my French, and as I intended to sing 'The Bee' song I asked Maurice what was the French for a bee. He said 'L'abeille and so I asked him what a busy bee was and he said 'L'abeille, très occupée,' which I knew wouldn't fit the music at all. Anyway, at the concert, with all the élite of Paris in the audience, I made my entrance and said, 'Monsieur le President, Mesdames et Messieurs, je suis le premier comique d'Angleterre – je pense! Mais je parle français mais un petit pois.' I meant, of course, to say 'petit peu'. It got the biggest (unintentional) laugh of the evening.

We spent a couple more days in Paris and were preparing to go to some other places where our lads were stationed, when all of a sudden we were told to pack quickly and go to the airport. Rumours that the Germans were preparing an advance were in the air and at the airport there were dozens of people waiting for transport back to England. Gracie, Jack and I received V.I.P. treatment and were at the head of the queue. (Dickie was missing, lost, somewhere in Paris!) An old four-engined de Havilland plane limped in, flying on three engines; we got on board and managed to reach Northolt in one piece. Within the next few hours, the Germans had started their blitzkreig. We got out just in time – the 'phoney' war was over.

THE BAND WAGGON film was released (or more likely put on parole) at the Leicester Square Theatre in January 1940. It was enthusiastically received by the producers, distributors, box-office managers, and the public in general. The critics were not quite so impressed – theirs was modified rapture, though not unkind. C. A. Lejeune wrote, '*Band Waggon* is as much like a picture as a village bun-fight.' About me she said:

> This is 'Big's' first film and he is still not quite certain of his medium. He tends to mug and over-act. Accustomed to the footlights and the microphone, he hasn't realised yet how the camera amplifies every grimace and gesture. But the promise of real comedy is there. The little man has pathos. Like all the great clowns, from Grock to Chaplin, he knows how to command sympathy as well as laughter. You laugh with Arthur Askey – never at him.

Another critic wrote, 'If Arthur Askey had a little pathos in his make-up, he might prove to be a reasonable comedian.' Well – you can't win 'em all!!

I was unable to attend the première of the film in London as I was still in pantomime at Birmingham, and I saw the trade show there. It received many laughs, probably because I took along the entire cast from the pantomime and they were all on my side. At this time I was also making records for H.M.V. where I had a contract for two years to make two records every month. Apart from the 'Bees', 'Moths', 'Seagulls' (even the 'Death Watch Beetles') I recorded the more commercial records of the time. I was the first to sing 'We're going to hang out the washing on the Siegfried Line' (for which I was put on Hitler's Black List), 'Run Rabbit Run', 'Kiss me goodnight, sergeant-major' – anything that was topical.

During the run of the pantomime, I had a call from Jack Taylor, the north country impresario. He wanted me to do the summer season for him at the Opera House, Blackpool, the newest and biggest (seating over 3,000) theatre in the country. He wanted Dickie Murdoch as well, and he had discussed the matter with Jack Hylton, as he wanted to call the show 'Blackpool's Own Band Waggon'. Hylton had a confidential chat with me and said, 'You'll find Jack Taylor a most amusing and genial fellow, until you work for him.' He also said he had heard that Taylor had booked Frank Randle for the proposed summer show. Randle was a tremendous favourite with the Blackpool audiences – deservedly so – but was well known for his eccentricities. Hylton said, 'If he's in the show, you won't live with him; he'll wipe the floor with you on his own ground.' Hardly an encouraging comment, but blunt and to the point. Anyway I met Taylor at the Queen's Hotel, we had a meal together and sure enough he had me in stitches with his tales of Frank Randle, Dave Morris, Albert Modley and all those great north country comics. He told me he had booked the Albert Sandler trio for the summer show, also Sid Seymour and his Mad Hatters, Wild Willie West and McGinty, fifty dancers, and several smaller acts. I asked him bluntly, 'Have you booked Frank Randle?' and when he said he had, I said he had better count me out as Jack Hylton had warned me I wouldn't survive in the show in competition with Randle. 'Oh – you needn't worry about that,' said Taylor. 'If you don't want Frank on the bill with you, I can put him in my other show on the South Pier, or send him on tour with one of my revues.' He then asked me how I would fancy having

Norman Evans instead. This I agreed to with alacrity. I knew Norman as a great comedian, and as a most lovable man. So all was signed and sealed: I was to appear at the Opera House for the summer, at a salary of £350 a week. My earning capacity was now more realistic.

We rehearsed at Blackpool, and Dickie turned up safely. I hadn't seen him since Paris. He had missed the plane out and had had a hell of a job returning to England. Rehearsals started and I began to see the real Jack Taylor, a real martinet and not a very pleasant one at that. He used to keep us at it until the small hours of the morning – there were no Equity rules to save us in those days. Jack Taylor's solution to the Randle problem wasn't as easy as he thought. Frank had a contract for the Opera House, and it was the Opera House he'd play, and nowhere else. So Taylor had to pay him about £150 a week for doing nothing. To make matters worse, Randle used to stand by the stage-door every night, with a bottle of Guinness in his hand, in order irritate Taylor.

Following Dunkirk, there were many army lads around Blackpool in hospital blue, and one evening I had a visit from an army major who told me there was a hospital at Preston, full of lads who were starved of entertainment and could I help? I was only too happy, considering all that they had been through, and I organised the whole show to go to Preston one afternoon in three coaches. All the principals, dancers, and orchestra members were only too willing to do their bit. There was quite a good stage at the hospital so we were able to give them almost the whole of the Opera House show, and were we a great success with the boys in blue! We had tea in the commandant's room before leaving for Blackpool, and he took me on one side and thanked me sincerely for organising the show. I said, 'We don't want thanking – after all that these lads did for us at Dunkirk.' He paused, then said, 'Oh, none of them have been farther than under the Pier at Blackpool – this is a V.D. hospital!' Was I popular with the rest of the company when the news leaked out!

I had taken a house for the season near Lytham. We found a school for Anthea and St Annes Old Links were quite handy for my almost daily game of golf. At least we were away from the bombing and life was quite pleasant. One bomb did fall near the station at

Blackpool – it was one the Jerry pilot had forgotten to release over Liverpool – and our only regret was that it missed Jack Taylor!

Throughout the season, I had been getting boils in the most peculiar places and the doctor said I was completely run down and must take things easier. Eventually the boils turned into carbuncles. I had as many as six at a time, and they were agony. But I kept on until the very last week, when I had to give in and George Formby took over for me. I had met George on and off throughout the summer – he would pop into my room for a quick drink if he could shake Beryl off for a few seconds. What a life he had with her. There was no doubt as to who was the boss. Almost the same situation as poor Arthur Lucan with that harridan Kitty McShane, though not quite so physical. George himself was a nice simple fellow. What his talent was is hard to define, but he was magic on the stage, and his films were popular all over the world. But Beryl ruled him with a rod of iron.

The last time I saw George was when he was appearing at the Queen's Theatre, Blackpool, for the summer with Yana, the singer, with whom he had fallen in love. Beryl was dying, and I'll never forget George saying to me, 'Arthur, I've just had the happiest eight weeks of my life.' I asked about Beryl and he said, 'Oh, she's just been on the phone wanting another bottle of whisky.' I asked who was looking after her and he said, 'Oh, Fred (who was his dresser) stays with her until I get home, then I have to set about changing the dirty sheets and trying to look after her.' A short while later she died, a happy release for her and a happier one for George. And yet for years they had been looked upon by the public as almost the Romeo and Juliet of show business. At the end of George's act he used to say to the audience, 'I'll bet you're all dying to see Beryl – well, here she is.' On would come Beryl looking very surprised as the conductor handed her a bouquet of flowers. After the show the flowers were then dusted and freshened up ready to be handed up at the second house, and again the next day if they would last. When I was in Australia, I went to a party and as I started to sit down the hostess shouted, 'Don't you dare sit there, Beryl Formby sat in that chair,' and all the guests laughed their heads off. Beryl was very royalty-conscious and she'd told the

Aussies how they had been to Windsor Castle, and as she was leaving, she tripped over the carpet. The Queen (now the Queen Mother) caught her by the arm and said, 'Oh, that was unfortunate,' to which Beryl replied, 'Oh no, it's lucky really. There's a theatrical superstition that if you trip as you are leaving a place, you are always invited back again.' And (according to Beryl) the Queen said, 'Ah well, you know where we live!'

I left Blackpool and took my family and my carbuncles to Port Merrion (Penrhyndeudraeth) in Wales to have a much-needed rest. Jack Hylton and his family came with us and I can remember sitting in the hotel, listening to the gloomy news each evening and wondering what was going to happen to us all. The bombing in London was on the increase, and I hated the thought of taking May and Anthea there when I had to return to begin my next film, *The Ghost Train*. Jack said he was sending his family up to Lakeside in Lake Windermere, so I decided to do the same, much against May's wishes. Anyway, off they went and Jack and I travelled in the opposite direction to London, where we had our first real taste of the bombing. It was so bad that most of the cast at the Shepherds Bush studios had beds in their dressing rooms, as the alert was usually on by the time we had finished shooting each day and was still on when we commenced work at eight o'clock the following morning.

We finished the film in early December 1941 and I travelled by car to Lakeside to collect May and Anthea. I arrived on the Saturday and the following day we drove to Leeds, where I was to appear in the *Jack and Jill* pantomime which had been such a success at Birmingham the previous Christmas. The cast was the same with the exception of the principal boy and Billy Bennett, who had decided there was an easier way of earning a living than doing a three-hour pantomime twice a day. Again the pantomime was a big success, though we were showing at odd times on account of the blackout. On one day a week we even had a morning performance and often started the evening show at five o'clock.

Dave and Jo O'Gorman asked me if I had ever seen the City of Varieties Music Hall. I said I hadn't, but would like to. So one night we went along there and saw a revue entitled *This Is The Show*, the first letter of each word being in large bold type! Up to that week, the company had been playing a pantomime *Dick Whittington*, obviously a 'do-it-yourself' job to cash in over the Christmas period. They had now reverted to the revue, but the comedian (obviously well sozzled) had forgotten this fact. He came on stage and said, 'I am waiting here for sweet Alice Fitzwarren . . .', suddenly realised the panto was over and quickly changed mid-sentence to 'I mean – a funny thing happened to me on the way to the theatre tonight!'

His act was followed by a comedy sketch and then it was time for the main attraction. The compère came on and said, 'Well, now as a change from the ridiculous to the sublime, we have great pleasure in presenting "La Belle Cleo" in her world-famous poses representing classic paintings of our time. Her first study will be "Love locked out".' Up went the curtain and there was a hefty blonde lady (I imagined her playing Dick in the panto), displaying her naked back to the audience, while holding on to a door which was being visibly supported by two stagehands at the back. She had played the previous sketch obviously dressed only in a frock and a pair of shoes – and there she was now, displaying the biggest bottom in the world for all the artistic members of the audience to see. There was a black-out, after sufficient time had elapsed for all and sundry to have an eyeful, then the compère reappeared and said, 'And now, "September Morn".' The lady – greatly daring – was now almost giving the audience a full frontal view, such erotica in Leeds! And so it went on until we had seen six of the world's greatest pictures, and a selection of feminine curves, bulges, and varicose veins.

Whenever I visit the City of Varieties to record *The Good Old Days*, I think fondly of 'La Belle Cleo'. She's probably Mrs Ramsbottom of Bacup now. Incidentally, to finish his act the comedian sang a funny song about the human anatomy. The chorus went: 'We all know what our ears and eyes and nose are for, we know what our arms and legs are for as well.' It went on, taking in all points south, and finished with the punch line of all time: 'But the dimple in your tummy's just to hold the salt and pepper when you're eating fish and chips in bed!'

Jack Hylton told me he had bought a house just outside Oxford which had a two-bedroomed gardener's cottage adjoining. This he offered me for May and Anthea. I immediately accepted as I had been worried about where they could go while I was making yet another film in London. So when the pantomime finished, we travelled to Little Milton and took up residence in the heart of the country with the Hylton family up in the 'big house'. We grew all our own fruit and vegetables and 'came by' a lot of eggs, butter, and the like from friendly neighbours. Anthea started boarding school at Bletchley (this was where the Upper Chine School from the Isle of Wight had been evacuated). Coincidentally, I had always said in my Isle of Wight concert party days that I would like Anthea to go to that particular school, if I could afford it.

So I returned to London and Lime Grove again to start shooting my latest epic, wittily entitled *I Thank You*. Most of the twelve films I eventually made have appeared on the telly at some time or other, but not this one. And if a picture is too bad for television you know it must be a stinker, so enough said! After the film was completed, Dickie left to join the R.A.F. We had had a very happy and successful association together in radio, concert party, Music Halls, and films and I was sorry to see my old playmate depart. We talked of resuming *Band Waggon* when things were back to normal, but during his war service he teamed up with Kenneth Horne, the outcome of which was *Much Binding in the Marsh*, which ran for about ten years. So *Band Waggon* was finally laid to rest. In the ensuing years, I did several radio series, but none of them reached the peak of *Band Waggon*. They were:

1940   *Big's Broadcast*, which was broadcast from Bangor, North Wales
1942   *Big Time* with Florence Desmond and Jackie Hunter
1945   *Forever Arthur* with Kenneth Horne
1949   *How do you do?* (another of my catchphrases)
1952   *Arthur's Inn* with Kenneth Horne and Barbara Mullen
1954   *Hello playmates* with Bob Monkhouse and Denis Goodwin
1957   *Askey Galore*
1959   *The Arthur Askey Show*.

In addition I have guested on many other radio shows and have recently broadcast two series of *Do you Remember?*, in which I stir the mothballs and play old 78 recordings of some of the old timers about whom I have a story to tell. And there is, of course, the perennial *Does the Team Think?* with Jimmy Edwards, Ted Ray, Cyril Fletcher, and Mac Hobley. In my opinion the listeners don't hear the best part of this show. We record for an hour and our producer, Ted Taylor, then cuts out the more bawdy parts. But at least our reputations remain intact (the best place for them).

After the departure of dear old 'Stinker' I toured the Halls for a few weeks and wherever I played, the Jerries seemed to follow me. I should never have recorded 'We're going to hang out the washing'! I returned to London to commence film number five, *Back Room Boy*. This had quite a good story concerning – but you must have seen it on television. If you haven't, don't worry, you will! It will be hailed as one of the 'Great movies of our time' and the excuse for showing it will be 'another chance to see'. But it was not a bad little movie and I had Googie Withers as my leading lady. When the picture was finished, I started rehearsing for the *Jack and Jill* pantomime again. Jack Hylton had bought the production from Emile Littler and we were to present it at the Palace Theatre, Cambridge Circus. And what a cast we had: Florence Desmond (Dessie) was the principal boy and her legs matched up to her talent. She was, without doubt, the finest impersonator of them all. She not only sounded like, but also looked like Marlene Dietrich, Bette Davis, Katherine Hepburn, Vera Lynn or whomever she 'took off'. She wore a short cloak over her shoulders 'as the Prince of Sylvania' and she removed that and put it around her waist to form a skirt to do her act. She was a joy to work with – a true professional.

Another member of the cast was 'Monsewer Eddie Gray'. I have often been asked, 'Who was the funniest comedian you ever met or worked with?' and without hesitation I say 'Eddie Gray'. I had a long and happy association with him and at one time I even refused to go out on tour without him. His act was funny enough with his fractured French and his juggling, but off stage he was hilarious. I have always said, 'If I ever write my life story, Eddie will have two chapters to himself.' Yet when it comes to writing it down, it's impossible to get his fantastic humour across.

He was always ready for a practical joke. I remember on one occasion coming off the North Pier, Blackpool, after a show, when

Eddie stopped by a pillar box. It was midday and the usual lunch-time crowds were milling around. Eddie went up to the pillar box and began shouting through the letter slot: 'Well how did you get in there in the first place?' He then put his ear to the slot and carried on a bizarre conversation, finishing with, 'Well don't panic. I'll fetch the fire brigade!' By the time we moved off there were about five hundred people waiting to see the rescue. Another classic incident was when we were at the Palladium. There was a ventrilo-quist on the bill who used to leave his life-size dummy, covered in a sheet, on the side of the stage overnight. One evening Eddie took it under the stage, sat it on the musician's lavatory, and removed the light bulb. During the short interval the members of the or-chestra waited and waited for this stranger to complete his ablutions. Eventually they all had to return to the pit, realising they would have to 'hang on' until the end of the show. This meant we sped through the second half of the programme and all went home early. What an under-rated comic genius Eddie Gray was!

The panto at the Palace was a huge success and we were packed twice a day despite the bombs. The Queen brought the two prin-cesses Elizabeth and Margaret to see their first pantomime and Dessie and I were invited to the Royal Box to meet them in the interval. Dessie went in first (with me close behind) and being the complete actress she was, she did the quickest and lowest curtsy of all time – she disappeared from sight! So did I because I tripped over her and landed flat on my face at the feet of the Queen. I have heard of people prostrating themselves in front of royalty, but this was ridiculous! The two young princesses said they were enjoying the pantomime and told us about their own pantomime at Windsor Castle, with Elizabeth playing the principal boy and Margaret the principal girl. It was my first brush with 'yer royals' and a very pleasant experience it was too. Later, in June, I appeared in a concert at Buckingham Palace and met the King for the first time. Other artistes on the bill were Bebe Daniels and Ben Lyon, Leslie Henson and Stanley Holloway, Harry Korris, Robbie Vincent and Cecil Frederick (of *Happidrome*), Jessie Matthews, Donald Peers, Anne Shelton, Jack Train, Elsie and Doris Waters, and the Western Brothers. What a bill! It was like a wartime Com-mand Performance.

While at the Palace one of the regular visitors to my dressing room was A. V. (Lord) Alexander, the First Lord of the Admiralty. He was actually in my room when he was called to the phone to be told the *Hood* had been sunk. He asked me back to Admiralty House to supper one night and I was very thrilled to see the inside of this historic building. I thought of all the famous people who had lived there through the years. All sorts of names ran through my head (a lot of them quite inaccurate!) and it gave me a great feeling of patriotic nostalgia. We had supper in a smallish room with Esther, Lady Alexander, who was absolutely sweet. She asked me if I would like to see the dining room where all the big banquets had taken place in the old days. It was a magnificent room and, being Christmas time, it had a lot of festoons, streamers and balloons hung around the place. Being wartime, Christmas decorations were hard to come by, so I said, 'You were lucky to get these, weren't you?' and she said, 'Oh, Bert got them from the Co-op!' At one time 'Bert' (A. V.) had been the head of that organisation. I did several shows for Lady Alexander, who was very interested in raising funds for Comforts for the Navy. One night Jack Hylton collected Florence Desmond, Eddie Gray and me in his car to go to one of these affairs, which was only a mile or so away in the West End. Because of this, he received a summons for the misuse of petrol. The authorities at that time were looking for a big name to set an example of what could happen if you were caught using petrol illegally. Jack was really frightened – he thought he was going 'inside', but he knew 'where the body was buried' and got away with it. The one who caught it was Ivor Novello. I was invited to his coming-out party at the Savoy which was a gay yet very sad occasion. Ivor felt it deeply and I am certain that the experience contributed to the cause of his early death.

The pantomime ran until the end of April 1942 and I spent a little time relaxing with May and Anthea at Little Milton. Then I did several shows for ENSA, usually at air bases, well off the beaten track. One of these was at Benson Aerodrome on a freezing Sunday night. The concert was held in a hangar with a communal dressing room for males and females rigged up in a corner. The ladies all complained of the cold and decided to work in their fur coats, but not Evelyn Laye. She asked us to turn our backs while she got into a very low-cut dress, and went on to the stage with goose-pimples on her goose-pimples to show the lads a bit of femininity. Good for 'Boo'.

After a short tour of the Halls, I had to report at the studios for my next epic entitled *King Arthur was a Gentleman*. My leading lady was Evelyn Dall, the original American blonde bombshell, and a real dolly girl she was too. Also in the cast were Anne Shelton, Max Bacon, Jack Train, Peter Graves, and Ronnie Shiner. I can't remember much about the picture, but it had a good ending. The story was that I'd joined the Army and I was always telling the boys in the hut about King Arthur and the Knights of the Round Table. We were stationed somewhere in Cornwall near Camelot, so the boys bought an old sword and buried it where I was sure to dig it up on manœuvres. I duly obliged and was thrilled to think I had found Excalibur – King Arthur's sword. I took it overseas with me and after a lot of comic (?) adventures, returned to England to find my girl had jilted me and everything else had gone wrong. Then my mates told me the sword was a phoney, so my whole world collapsed around me. The last scene in the film was of miserable me, sitting beside a lake, gazing at the sword. Eventually I stood up, gave the sword a dirty look and threw it into the lake. And guess what, a hand and arm appeared out of the water, grabbed the sword, waved it around three times and slowly drew it down into the lake until it disappeared from view. That will save you watching the film when it eventually reaches your television screen (there must be a copy of it somewhere!).

I was no longer sleeping in my dressing room; we had gone back to the Islington studios and there were not the same facilities there. So I decided that I would stay at the Savoy Hotel. If a bomb was to come down with my name on it, I was determined I would go out in style. I stayed there on and off for three years and, needless to say, I met very many interesting people of stage, screen, politics, commerce, even con-men and crooks – the whole gamut of high life. Living at the Savoy, I became quite a ponce, being invited to all kinds of functions that took place there. I remember letting the New Year in dancing with the famous Margot, Lady Asquith.

The pantomime, such a success at the Palace the previous Christmas, was to be repeated at His Majesty's Theatre, so I was rehearsing again with pretty much the same cast. We had a different principal girl, Kathleen Moody, very pretty with a lovely voice. She was then engaged to a rather small-time agent who had at one time been the World's Champion Charleston dancer. They later married and honeymooned at the Imperial Hotel, Torquay. They were going to stay for a week till they saw the prices, so shortened their honeymoon to two days. They are now Sir Lew and Lady Grade and just as nice and unassuming now as they were then. By the way, my principal boy in the Birmingham panto is now Lady Littler, and Carole Lynn who was in *The Ghost Train* (and a principal girl with me later) is now Lady Delfont. So, girls, if you want to get a title, work with 'Big-hearted Arthur' and your dreams will come true!

After the pantomime finished at His Majesty's, I started work on my next film, *Miss London, Ltd*, with Evelyn Dall, Ann Shelton, and several of the cast from my previous picture. It was in the nature of a musical, had some good songs by Manning Sherwin, and was directed by Val Guest. When the picture was released, the film critic of *The Sunday Pictorial* gave it eight out of ten, which I thought was about right. However, the *Daily Sketch* critic, Elspeth Grant, wrote 'Mr Val Guest has succeeded in lifting an Arthur Askey vehicle out of the "films to be suffered". Nice work!' I thought this was a bit of a back-handed compliment, but she had spelt my name correctly and that's really all that matters.

Anyway, it didn't stop me from starting right away on my next epic, *Bees in Paradise*. This was the story of four airmen – Peter Graves, Ronald Shiner, Max Bacon, and myself – who crash-landed on a semi-tropical island which was entirely inhabited by females. Males there were only used for procreation, and having fulfilled their function they were thrown off the top of a cliff into the sea. All good clean fun for the kiddies! The script, lyrics, and direction were by Val Guest, and it was Jean Kent's first film.

The bombing was still very bad in London and we were delighted to hear we were to go to Torquay on location. It was the nearest they could get to a 'tropical island' atmosphere, so the whole unit moved there and took over the Torbay Hotel. We all had a wonderful uninterrupted night's sleep and the following day (a Sunday) set off for the cliffs at Marychurch to start shooting. On the way we passed a church and saw all the kiddies going in to Sunday School. There was one little coloured girl among them and I wittily said, 'I didn't know Hutch had been here.' Everybody laughed. We were so relieved to get away from London, we laughed at anything.

We had just set up for the first shot when there was an air-raid warning. A local who was standing nearby (they come up out of holes once they see a film camera) said, 'Oh – doan 'ee worry. We get these 'ere alarums all the toime, but nowt ever 'appens.' I looked out over the bay and saw fifteen Jerry planes flying within a few feet of the water. As they approached the headland, they split up into two sections. One went over the town itself and the other came directly for where we were standing, dropping bombs and firing machine-gun bullets. All hell broke loose. There was nowhere to shelter, so we all threw ourselves to the ground, and I had seventeen-stone Max Bacon on top of me. The cannon shells ripped up the earth all round us and I was badly cut on the face with flying gravel. After about two minutes of ear-splitting noise (the anti-aircraft guns had joined in) there was silence except for the fading drone of the aircraft engines as they headed back to the Channel Islands, from where they had come. There was no more shooting that day, from either aircraft or film cameras. We started to walk back to Torquay, passing what was left of the church where we had seen the kiddies a few minutes earlier. They were now carrying out the little bodies; quite a number had been killed. We walked down Union Street in Torquay, which was ankle-deep in glass and debris, finally reaching the hotel. I found two machine-gun bullet holes in my bedroom wall and had treatment for my bloody face.

It was reported in the papers – 'Arthur Askey injured in air-raid' – so my mother was down from Southport before the ink was dry! We all sat down to dinner that evening and reflected on the nearest squeak I was to have during the whole war. And, I'm sorry to say, the film that was made was not worth risking one's life for!

One day, during the filming in London, I was asked if I would go to the gramophone studios in Abbey Road as soon as I had finished shooting. When I got there everyone was very excited. Rudolph Hess had landed in England and a song had been written to celebrate the event, and who better to record it than me! It went like this:

> Thanks for dropping in – Mister Hess,
> We've told your friends to note your new address.
> They've heard you've got here safely in Berlin and in
>   Rome
> So put away your parachute and make yourself at
>   home.
> Thanks for dropping in – Mister Hess,
> Forgive the small announcement in the Press.
> Had you told us you were coming
> And informed us where you'd land
> We would certainly have had a big reception nicely
>   planned
> With a carpet and some streamers
> And Jack Hylton and his Band.
> Thanks for dropping in – thanks for popping in,
> What a nice surprise – Mister Hess.

The song had a belting tune and the record was rushed out to the dealers as soon as it was printed. Unfortunately, it was rushed back just as quickly – by order of the Government. They thought it was undiplomatic to make fun of the enemy, thereby foreshadowing Noël Coward's 'Don't let's be beastly to the Germans'. The newspapers got hold of the story – I saw to that – and berated those in High Places. Hannen Swaffer, then a very important man of Fleet Street, made a big fuss about it, and rightly so.

With *Bees in Paradise* in the can, I had now finished my eight-picture contract and was itching to do what I had come into the business for – a musical comedy. And my luck was in. Stanley Lupino had written a sequel to his highly successful *Lady Behave* at His Majesty's Theatre but he had health problems and was unable to tackle his new show *The Love Racket*. Poor Stanley, he was a great musical comedy comedian and, in addition, always wrote the shows in which he appeared. Bobby Howes took over for him in *Lady Behave* and Stanley never worked again; in fact he died shortly afterwards. So Jack Hylton started casting and arranging for me to star in *The Love Racket*, to be produced at the Opera House, Manchester, in September 1943.

During the waiting period, I had a couple of weeks with my wife and daughter at Little Milton, then did a tour of shows for the forces. I flew up to Scapa Flow for the Navy and had the thrill of dining on board H.M.S. *Duke of York* with six admirals, including my host Sir Bruce (later Lord) Fraser. I then went south to Portsmouth where I was to do a broadcast to all the warships lying in the Solent. I travelled by train from Waterloo and arrived at Portsmouth Harbour station where, to my amazement, I was met by a guard of honour. I didn't know whether to salute or do a comic trip; anyway I passed along the line with reasonable dignity. It was only after the show (and a lot of naval hospitality) that I heard the full story. The Wren in the signal office had made a mistake and they were not expecting 'ASKEY' but 'MAISKI', the Russian Ambassador! It reminded me of the time I attended a cocktail party given by Sir Noel Curtis-Bennett at his home in Portland Place. Among the guests were Clement Attlee, Sir Albert Atkey, and Arthur Askey. The guest list sounded like the old *Happidrome* signature tune 'There's Attlee, and Atkey, and me!' During the evening the phone kept ringing and over the hubbub of conversation somebody would shout 'Mister Attlee/Atkey/Askey wanted on the phone' and the three of us would arrive together and sort out who the call was for. It was usually for Clem, I might add.

I was asked to do a show at Ford Aerodrome on the Sussex coast one Sunday night, together with The Crazy Gang and Florence Desmond. When we arrived at the aerodrome gates, a very officious sergeant refused to let us in as we hadn't got passes. We were all arguing with him and on the point of calling the whole thing off when Eddie Gray arrived, gave the Nazi salute, and said to the sergeant, 'I haf called mit a message from the Führer – heil Hitler!' The sergeant fell about, and let Eddie in! We all got in eventually and gave the boys a wonderful show, but throughout the evening the alert kept going and in the end we were left with an audience of about a dozen ground staff. Each time the alarm went, several young pilots and their crews would jump up and dash out of the hangar. Not even Bud Flanagan's appeal 'Come back, lads – we're not that bad' could stop them. This was the pattern of things at all the R.A.F. concerts I did and one could not help wondering when those brave young chaps went off, just how many would return. It made our war effort appear a very feeble affair and I always felt the thanks we received from the C.O.s at the end of the shows were very unnecessary.

THE LOVE RACKET opened in Manchester on 9 September 1943. Among the cast were Roy Royston, Carol Raye, Valerie Tandy, Finlay Currie, and Hugh Morton, and the musical score was by Noel Gay. The show was a rip-roaring success and I was in my element. One critic wrote:

> Arthur Askey (shorn of his famous 'Ay thank yew') is the star, and of him I can only say 'Go and see him for yourself or you'll be sorry when your friends tell you what you missed.' His vitality is endless. He makes his fellow artists laugh a good deal, but happily not quite so much as the audience, or the show would hardly be able to go on.

We ran for two weeks in Manchester, then two weeks at the Royal Court Theatre, Liverpool. I stayed with my parents at Southport and, needless to say, my mother came to every performance. I had a further week at the New Theatre, Oxford, and then, the big moment, our first night facing a West End audience at the Victoria Palace.

When we went to Manchester, the show had been given a licence by the Lord Chamberlain but we had since introduced a new scene during the tour. The scene was based on Roy Royston and myself pretending to be authors. I decided my author should look like George Bernard Shaw and Roy, even more ridiculously, thought his should look like Shakespeare. So we met on an empty stage and circled around each other, me dressed as Shaw complete with beard and knickerbockers and Roy with cloak, bald pate, and quill pen. The witty dialogue opened as follows:

Roy (with a deep bow): 'May I bid you a good morrow, gentle sire.'
Me: 'Not bloody likely!'
Roy: 'Are you Shaw?'
Me: 'I'm certain.'

and continued in the same vein.

When we arrived to open in London, Hylton at the last minute remembered to send the script of the new scene to the Lord Chamberlain. Back it came saying we could do it, providing Bernard Shaw's permission to impersonate him was obtained. A script was sent to him, and on the morning of production Hylton received a postcard, written in red ink, which just said 'No. G.B.S.' This caused real consternation, as the scene was now such an important part of the show and a big laughter-raiser.

Jack found out that Shaw was at his flat in Whitehall Court, so together with William Mollison, the producer, he sallied forth to see if he could persuade G.B.S. to relent. Back he came about an hour later, very whitefaced, and said he had not succeeded. Shaw was adamant. As it was I who would have suffered most if the scene was lost, I was determined to have a go myself. So off I went to Whitehall Court, rang the bell, and was greeted by a housekeeper. I started to ask her if there was any chance of my seeing Mr Shaw when a voice called, 'Who is it?' and she replied, 'Mr Arthur Askey.' 'Tell him to come in,' said the light Irish voice, and there I was – in the master's presence. He was sitting behind a big desk, but rose as I went in and shook hands with me. He then told me how much he had enjoyed hearing me on the wireless at which I began to feel a little more confident. He then said, 'Now – what can I do for you?' The script was in front of him, so I pointed to it and said, 'I've come to see you about this.' He said, 'Oh, this is schoolboy rubbish!' to which I replied, 'Well, if you've heard me on the wireless, you know that's what my humour is – schoolboy rubbish.' 'But not as bad as this,' he said, and started reading the script aloud. He really made it sound awful. I said, 'Well, this scene where I impersonate you is one of the high spots of the show.' He retorted, 'If this is one of the high spots, I'd hate to see the low spots.' And he added, 'You know Shakespeare wasn't a bad writer either, but he's not here to defend himself!' I was absolutely fascinated with the man, his keen wit and the easy way he talked, and I wish I had taken a tape recorder with me. I had been with him for an hour and the time had come to say a reluctant 'Goodbye' to the great man. As we got to the front door, I made one last appeal for his permission to do the sketch. He looked at me and said, 'No, I won't, but there's not the slightest reason why you shouldn't do it, because I won't be coming to see it!' So I rushed back to the theatre and we decided to take a chance and keep the scene in. But for the first few weeks, every time I went on stage, I had a look around the stalls to see if there was any sign of that famous white beard.

We opened to the usual first-night audience of show biz personalities, critics, hangers-on, agents, and gallery first-nighters. After our success in the provinces, we found the going a little tough until halfway through the first act when I had to carry a female bust off stage. I had quarrelled with my stage wife and said, 'Okay – if that's the way you feel about it, I'm going off with another woman.' I picked up the bust, swung round to say my exit line and caught the head on the scenery. It rolled into the middle of the stage, so I returned, picked it up, looked at it and said, 'Never lose your head on a first night!' An audience loves anything which goes wrong, so this resulted in much laughter. From then on, the show really went with a bang. In the interval Jack Hylton, Bill Mollison, and everybody concerned came into my dressing room full of congratulations – 'You ought to hear what they're saying in the bars,' etc. So I made my entrance in the second act full of confidence, really cocky, and started some dialogue with my stage wife, Peggy Carlisle, which led into a duet. We had been going about five minutes when a lone figure came slowly down the centre aisle, limping on a stick. My Music Hall instinct came to the fore and I stopped the dialogue and asked the gent, 'Wouldn't they serve you?', 'I'll tell you what's happened up to now', etc. He sat down in his seat on the end of the fourth row and after enquiring if he was 'quite comfy', I got on with the show. All this received a sort of shocked laughter from the audience and I felt I had dropped a clanger somewhere along the line. I soon found out how. When I made my exit Hylton said, 'Now you've done it. That was James Agate – he'll crucify us in *The Times* tomorrow.' Agate was the most feared critic of his time, and it was the first occasion I had come under his scrutiny.

In Agate's notice of the show the following day, he devoted a whole column to Hecuba, Hector, Lear, Cordelia, The Duchess of Malfi, Kean, Macready, Mrs Siddons, Otway's Jaffier, Pierre and Belvidera, Byron, Falstaff, Sir Toby, Lamb, Holofernes, Sir Nathaniel, Don Adriano, Sir Hugh Evans, and Doctor Caius. He then wrote, 'What, in descending scale, about our Music Hall comedians?' and then went on about Dan Leno, Arthur Roberts, Charlie Chaplin, Little Tich, and George Robey. He analysed each of these, finishing by saying of Robey that when he came on the stage as a leering toper, his face all bubukles and knobs and flames of fire, his mind 'manured and nourished with jests', you felt 'that invention and not memory was at work'. Agate then went on to say:

Does one feel this about Mr Arthur Askey? Before saying that I personally do not, let me concede that the fact that a match does not strike on my box may be as much the fault of the box as of the match. The impression I get from Mr Askey's acting is that it is synthetic, in the sense that somebody invents a joke to which he then gives shape by pretending to walk like a chimpanzee or by putting on a funny hat. I am prepared for the objection that half, perhaps three-quarters of this comedian's humour is self-invented; I must still maintain that as a comedian he fails to convey the creative sense. Is this perhaps because Mr Askey, who never stops calling attention to his lack of inches, insists a little too much on the homunculosity of the homunculus? On the stage it seems to me that this comedian's humour is physical and accidental rather than of the mind and integral. I feel I have not got at the whole truth about a performer whom half the world regards as a great clown, one who, on the radio, discards the visual appeal and is, I am told, very funny. I hasten to add that on Tuesday night an immense audience found him funnier still.

I still don't know what all that really means. But despite James Agate, the rest of the critics were most eulogistic about the show and we knew we were booked for a long run. I used to meet Agate at the Savage Club – he wasn't a bad old stick really – and I would kid him that probably nobody had read his notice anyway: 'My fans read the *Daily Worker*!' He was a homosexual and had a menage à trois with his chauffeur and his house-man valet. The story goes that one day he walked slowly down the steps of his house, got into the car, and found he had left his walking stick behind. He told the chauffeur to get it for him, and the chauffeur ran up the steps, knocked at the door, and lisped to the house-man, 'She's forgotten her wand!'

The Love Racket ran for about a year at the Victoria Palace and then we took it on tour, playing all the big cities with equal success. We also played at various army camps such as Catterick, Salisbury, and Aldershot. At the latter place, the show didn't seem to go as well as usual. It was only after the curtain came down that we were told the audience consisted entirely of French Canadians! I also did Sunday shows for the troops on my own. Basil Dean of ENSA asked if I would do a 'special' at Belle Vue, Manchester, with Gertrude Lawrence. The audience consisted of four thousand British soldiers and four thousand Americans. I was thrilled to meet 'Gertie' and we went around the fairground together on the swings, roundabouts, river-caves, etc. while waiting to rehearse with Geraldo's orchestra. We lost all idea of time and when we eventually got back to the hall, the band had disappeared. However, we both had our own pianists, so we survived. But what a lovable character she was, and what an artiste.

Hylton brought *The Love Racket* back to London for the Christmas period and we did eight weeks at the Adelphi Theatre. Then after another short tour, we arrived in the West End at the Princes

Theatre for yet another run. And despite the doodle-bug we still played to full houses. A bomb fell uncomfortably close to the theatre one evening just as Roy Royston and Valerie Tandy were doing a hectic tap dance. Roy didn't miss a beat, just looked up, gave the V-sign, and carried on dancing. When I got back to my dressing room I found all the windows blown in and my dresser badly cut about the face. He was quite a character – with a name like Pat Murphy, he had to be. He used to talk about 'lectic lights' and tell me he had seen a film in 'technical colour'.

I was very thrilled one matinée to find Leslie Henson sitting in a box. At the end of the show, I made a speech telling the audience how much I had admired Leslie and that I had come into the business hoping I would be like him some day. Leslie stood up and replied by saying how much he had 'enjoyed seeing Mister – er –'. He then referred to the programme to find my name, and said if he ever had another free afternoon, he would make a point of coming to see 'Mister – er – (referring to programme again) Archie Askew'. He was hysterically funny and went on so long that I told the company to sit down on the stage. This didn't stop him so I eventually went to the wings and got a bunch of keys. These I threw up to the box and asked Leslie if he'd lock up when he'd finished. Here was a genuine 'funny man' who didn't have to rely on script-writers. He could get many laughs by just rolling his cod-fish eyes or saying quite a straight line in his gravelly voice.

I bought a house in Sussex – on the downs, but near the sea – towards the end of 1944 and we moved in just before Christmas. It was a lovely house standing in about an acre and a half with a golf course at the back door. We had a gardener and grew all our own vegetables and fruit. The gardener used to arrive on his bike each morning with a suitcase which, he said, contained his lunch. We used to watch him pedalling away at the end of the day and from the angle at which he sat on his bike, we could tell the case was much heavier than it had been when he'd arrived! We had some friends coming to lunch one day, so May asked him to cut some asparagus. He presented her with half a dozen tatty stalks and said that was all there was. So I dashed down to the greengrocer in the village and asked for two or three bundles. I said, 'Is it really nice asparagus?' and the greengrocer replied, 'It should be – it's from your garden!'

I loved living in my own house for the first time though, as usual, I had to leave it more often than I wanted to go and earn my daily bread. We did a few more weeks touring with *The Love Racket* and then I was back on the Halls again.

Jack Hylton said he had found another musical comedy for me, an American show called *Follow the Girls*. I read the script and heard the score, even saw a film of it, and I knew it was for me. The principal comedy part had been played in the U.S.A. by Jackie Gleason, who looked more like Fred Emney than me, but size didn't matter. I knew I could do it. The leading lady was a night-club singer and who better to play the part than Evelyn Dall. The other characters were played by Wendy Toye, Hugh French, Jackie Billings, Vic Marlowe, etc., and we commenced rehearsals at the beginning of August 1945. We opened in Manchester, this time at the Palace, and again found we had a big success on our hands. After a couple of weeks at Liverpool and Blackpool, we opened at His Majesty's Theatre, London, on 26 October and ran for nearly two years. Many of the cast wilted and left during the long run – I had four different leading ladies – but I revelled in it. One of the things that makes me sick in our business is the way actors and actresses complain they can't do too long a run.

When Sir Herbert Beerbohm Tree built His Majesty's Theatre, he did himself proud. As well as a dressing room, he had a suite comprising a large drawing room and a bathroom. I wonder how he would have felt if he had known it was going to be occupied by a low-life comic like me – as I did in the pantomime, and during the long run of *Follow the Girls*. Jack Hylton's offices were up in the dome of the building, so naturally I saw a great deal of him. He usually brought visitors with him and I met Billy Rose, the famous Broadway producer (who said I was better than Jackie Gleason in the part – what a good judge of talent!), and also Frederick ('Fritzi') Loewe, the composer of the music for *Paint Your Wagon*, *Brigadoon*, and (later) *My Fair Lady*. He offered me a cigarette and I noticed he had a pill taped in his gold cigarette case. I asked him what it was for and he said that if ever he had a bad accident, or was struck down with an incurable disease, he would use this pill for his final exit. Ugh!

Lord Louis (now Earl) Mountbatten was in the audience one

140

night, in uniform with his rows of ribbon decorations. I made my last entrance in the show dressed as an admiral with dozens of medals pinned all over the front of my uniform, and the back as well. I looked at Lord Louis and said, 'Show you for the most', which got a big laugh, from him in particular. He came round to see me afterwards and had a drink in my – or shall I say Sir Herbert Tree's – drawing room. On this particular night, the safety curtain stuck after the interval. It was rising about half an inch a minute, so I nipped through the pass door, stood in front of the orchestra rails and told the audience we would recommence the show as soon as the girls' knees came into view. We started the second half all crouching like Groucho Marx until the safety curtain was reasonably clear.

In addition to the show, I was doing quite a lot of radio work, including *Forever Arthur*, which was recorded at the Paris Cinema in Lower Regent Street, just around the corner, after I'd finished two performances of *Follow the Girls*. And then there was usually a concert to cope with each Sunday. We did one at His Majesty's in aid of some charity or other and Jack Hylton told me there was a very funny comedian from the Windmill Theatre coming to do a turn. His name was Harry Secombe. I met him at rehearsal, took an instant liking to him, and told him he could use my (Sir Herbert's) dressing room. He was very nervous before the show and asked me if he could use my bathroom for a wash and a shave. His act in those days consisted of shaving himself while singing 'Figaro' and for this he used a safety razor, minus the blade. After he had shaved in my bathroom, he was so nervous that he forgot to remove the blade and in consequence, when he started his act, he cut himself very badly and there was blood all over the place. The audience was very perturbed, but not Harry. He kept on belting away, finishing up in a pool of blood, but with terrific applause. He really was a 'bloody' riot!

In 1946 I was invited to appear at my first Royal Variety Show. There had been one the previous year (the first after the war) and I was very piqued that I was not included, as I felt I had done so much for the variety theatre just before the outbreak of hostilities when Music Halls were closing all around the country. However, without being big-headed, I can honestly say I was the 'hit' of the 1946 show. On these occasions, there is always someone who 'stands out' and this time it was me. Naturally my mother was there as well as May and Anthea. After the show, flushed with success and having met the Royal Family, I joined my family to hear from them how good I had been. I thought Anthea seemed a bit quiet, so I asked her what she thought of the show. She replied, 'Do you know, Daddy – they didn't give me a spoon with my ice-cream!' To enable me to appear at the Royal Variety Show, my understudy had to play my part in *Follow the Girls* for that evening. It was one of the few times any understudy of mine has appeared. One of the reasons I am still in regular work is that I have always been reliable!

On the bill at the Variety Show was that wonderful comedian Sid Field, whose genius had just been discovered after years of touring the provinces. He was in a revue called *Strike a New Note* at the

Prince of Wales Theatre, and as there were two or three other acts from the same show in the programme, Val Parnell decided he would close the theatre for that evening. Parnell hated having to lose a show at the Prince of Wales, so to compensate he put on an extra matinée on the following Thursday. Immediately this was announced, every pro in London booked seats to see this new wonderful comedian Sid Field whom all the critics had raved about. Val took me on one side and told me that Sid was very nervous at the prospect of appearing in front of half the profession. Would I, he asked, go on before the matinée, chat up the audience, and tell them to behave like the ordinary public and not like critics, thus making things a bit easier for Sid. I was very happy (in fact eager) to do this, so on the Thursday afternoon, I went into Sid's dressing room and borrowed his 'Slasher Green' hat and long overcoat. You may remember Jerry Desmonde saying 'How much did you pay for that coat?', Sid replying 'A quid,' and Jerry saying 'You could have got a long one for that!'

The show opened with the usual dance routine from the girls, then on walked Jerry Desmonde. After he'd said a few words, I entered sideways with my head down and the hat pulled well over my eyes. The audience naturally thought it was Sid; most of them had never seen him before and didn't know if he was short or tall. There was a terrific round of applause. When I looked up and they saw it was me, they wondered what had happened. They were all there – Ivor Novello, Jack Buchanan, Bobby Howes, Leslie Henson, down to the smallest first turn comic – all had come to see what the fuss was about this Sid Field. I told them that we knew the audience was full of pros – 'In fact I've seen your baskets in the cloakroom and noticed a lot of unmarried mothers (landladies' daughters) waiting at the stage door.' I told them they were going to see a comedian who had definitely pinched all their best gags and bits of business, but he was all the critics had said about him and more. So would they behave like ordinary human beings who had paid for their seats and be entertained by the greatest comic find since me. Needless to say Sid came on and stormed them and it was the most exciting show I think I ever saw. At the end, Sid was obviously touched at the tremendous reception from his fellow artistes. He made a speech and thanked everybody from Val Parnell down to the wardrobe mistress. The orchestra, all his brother and sister

artistes, the stagehands – all were mentioned with the exception of
me. A few months later, Danny Kaye came over to play the Palladium and Val asked me if I would come and meet him in Sid's
dressing room after the show. I was very thrilled to meet Danny,
and Stan Laurel who was there too. Danny said he was feeling nervous about his Palladium début. I said to Val, 'Would you like me
to go and warm the audience up for him, like I did for you-know-
who?' Sid took the bait and said, 'Oh, my Gawd – I never thanked
you for doing that for me, Arthur. Do please forgive Sid-er-ney.
Tell you what. I'll buy you a settee and two easy chairs!' It's an old
cliché, but Sid's early death was a tremendous loss to the small list
of the all-time greats. Like Tony Hancock, his death seemed so unnecessary. And Sid's straight man, Jerry Desmonde – without doubt
the best 'feed' in the business, as Bob Hope, Norman Wisdom, and
I will vouch for – had an equally sad and tragic end.

I was honoured to take part in nine Command Performances –
1946, 1948, 1952, 1954, 1955, 1957, 1968, and 1972 at the Palladium, and one at the Opera House, Blackpool, also in 1955. The
latter was a hilarious affair. A special train from Euston carried most
of the artistes, dancers, and musicians, and lots of booze and food.
Charlie Naughton was 'streaking' (except for a guard's cap) along
the corridors about 4 a.m., knocking at all the sleeping compartment doors shouting 'Get that woman out of there' and other
Rabelaisian quips. We had breakfast on arrival and then rehearsed
all day prior to the show. There was a good smattering of northern
comics apart from myself – George Formby, Albert Modley, Norman Evans, Wilfred Pickles to mention a few. The Opera House
had no boxes, so a Royal Box was built on one side of the theatre.
Albert Modley got the biggest laugh of the night when he made his
entrance and bowed to the blank wall opposite. He looked up and
said, ''Allo – 'ave they gone?' He then turned the other way, looked
at the box, grinned and said, 'Flipping 'eck – I thowt yer'd 'opped it!'

We had supper after the show and I sat with Debbie Reynolds
and Eddie Fisher (two good Lancashire types!), who had been in
the show. Then we all packed into the train again, arriving at
Euston very bog-eyed in the small hours of the morning. I was also
in the Royal Show which never took place in 1956. We rehearsed all
over the weekend but on the Monday about four o'clock, Val Parnell

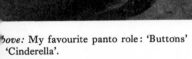

Above: My favourite panto role: 'Buttons' 'Cinderella'.

Lower Right: As Prince Ras Monolulu in 'The Kid from Stratford'.

Upper Right: In 'Babes in the Wood', at the Palladium, 1965.

Upper Left: Meeting Sir Robert Menzies at the Tivoli, Melbourne. *Upper Right:* With Aneurin Bevan and his wife Jenny Lee, at the opening night of 'Bet Your Life', 1951. *Middle Left:* Sold to Jack Hylton, 1952. *Middle Right:* With Hancock in the early days of Television. *Lower Right:* Causing a disturbance at Highbury.

Opposite, Bottom: Before your very eyes . . . Sabrina. *Top:* The finishing touches at Madame Tussauds: Mac Hobley looks on.

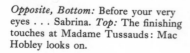

Left: Anthea's coming of age with Gracie Fields.
Below: Anthea and Bill, 2 March 1956.

called us all together and said the show had been cancelled on account of the Suez crisis. Liberace burst into tears and we were all feeling down in the mouth. However, Harry Secombe was in the current show at the Palladium and invited us all into his dressing room to drown our sorrows, which we well and truly did, with Jimmy Wheeler in tremendous form!

Royal Variety Shows sort out the thoroughbreds from the also-rans. Nerves play a big part. I've seen good artistes become gibbering idiots. I once walked Tony Hancock round the stage door area persuading him he was marvellous (which he was, once he got on stage). Our profession has more than its quota of 'big-heads' and the biggest one I ever met was Mario Lanza. At rehearsal, when told to bow to the Royal Box, he, with old-world courtesy, said 'Aw, shit!' He was offensive in every way all day, but when it was near to his turn, he began to weaken. He vainly looked for a friend to talk to, even the stagehands, but we all ignored him. And for my money, Harry Secombe who followed him sang twice as well.

At the most recent Royal Show I did, I was called in at the last moment to do a bit with Dickie Henderson and Teddy Piero. I hadn't had time to fraternise with the rest of the artistes, among whom were Carol Channing and Danny La Rue. I was walking backstage – very dimly lit – while the show was on and saw Danny in front of me. I pinched his bum and said 'Whatcher, mate,' the figure turned round and it was Carol Channing! She just said, 'You're a funny little feller,' (which I already knew!) and that was the end of it. She didn't know who I was from Adam, probably thought I was an Italian, though when you are my height, bottom-pinching is quite an effort!

When *Follow the Girls* finished – playing to good business to the end – I decided I must have a holiday. Another American musical comedy had been offered to me and as it was still on in New York I decided to go to America and see the show for myself. So with May and Anthea, I boarded the *Queen Elizabeth* at Southampton, very excited at the prospect of seeing something of the U.S.A.

We approached New York in the early hours of the morning, just as dawn was breaking, and it really was a fantastic sight to see the skyscrapers looming out of the morning mist. We berthed at Pier 90, then had the ritual of standing in the customs sheds, waiting for the baggage to be sorted out and placed opposite your initial. Eventually a tough-looking gum-chewing official came up to me, had a brief look at my cases and said, 'They tell me you're an English comedian?' I said I was and he looked me up and down and said, 'You don't look very funny to me, Mac,' chalked my bags and off he went. What a welcome!

We checked in at the Great Western Hotel on Madison Avenue and started three weeks of rubber-necking around New York. After our black-outs, to see Broadway lit up on our first night was a tremendous thrill. We went to see the show they wanted me to do. It was called *Sweethearts*, with music by Victor Herbert, but I didn't like it very much. The comedian was Bobby Clark (I had seen him in England as half of a double act called 'Clark and McCullough'). He was about my size and wore glasses painted on his face. He was very funny, but the show itself didn't appeal to me, so I sent Hylton a cable saying I was not interested. But the other shows I saw – *Oklahoma, Carousel, Annie Get Your Gun, Finian's Rainbow*, and *Brigadoon* – convinced me that the British type of musical comedy, traditionally featuring types like Jack Buchanan, Bobby Howes, Leslie Henson, Stanley Lupino, and yours truly, was coming to an end.

Brigadoon had just opened, and seats were very difficult to obtain. However, I saw it was presented by Billy Rose, so I telephoned him. No problem – he gave me the house seats and also invited me to see his *Diamond Horseshoe* production, featuring Olsen and Johnson. Apart from theatres, I went to the top night spots and also the big cinemas, including the Radio City Music Hall, the Roxy, and the Paramount, which all had lavish stage shows. At the Paramount I saw Xavier Cougat's Band. His vocalist was Dean Martin and he did a double act with a comic on the bill called Jerry Lewis – the first time they'd worked together. I also saw Fred Allen, Perry Como, Fred Waring, and several other radio shows being broadcast. All in all my holiday turned out to be a bonanza of all facets of American show business. I was asked to broadcast, but decided against it, and the only appearance I made was when I visited the Blue Angel night spot where Flo Desmond was appearing. She invited me up to take a bow and I cracked a few gags with her and found the American audience seemed to like what I said. Sophie Tucker was in the audience as well – she took a bow and nearly knocked me off the stage, for a laugh, of course. We spent the last evening at the opening of a Sophie Tucker season at the Copacabana.

What a holiday! It was a very tired Askey family that crawled back into the *Queen Elizabeth* after our three hectic weeks. May and Anthea didn't visit all the shows with me; they had a whale of a time looking at the shops in and around Fifth Avenue. Thank goodness they didn't spend too much as we were on a pretty tight budget (at that time you were only allowed to take a limited amount of money out of the country).

Back home, after a couple of weeks, I started rehearsals for yet another Hylton production. This was a revue called *High Tide* and it was to run for the whole of the summer at the Imperial Theatre, Brighton, now, alas, a Bingo hall. Florence Desmond and Eddie Gray were in the cast with me. It was a very happy show and as Dessie lived at Angmering, Eddie at Shoreham, and me within ten miles of Brighton, it suited us all very well, especially as it was a gorgeous summer. I did a lot with Eddie in the show and he used to dry me up night after night. Jack Hylton took me to one side and pointed out that I was supposed to be the star of the show, but what could I do? Just one look from Eddie could set me off – what an under-rated comic genius he was.

Anthea was at boarding school in the Isle of Wight at this time and the headmistress rang me one day to say that the Ventnor repertory company had asked if they could 'borrow' her for a week. They were presenting Emlyn Williams' play *Dear Evelyn* and they wanted a young girl of about twelve to play an important part. Anthea wanted to do it, chiefly because it meant she missed a lot of lessons for rehearsals, and had a week of late nights when the show was produced. She had a hired car (for which I was sent the bill!) each day for two weeks and felt she had arrived in the big time. The show had finished at Brighton by this time, so May and I went to see our talented daughter's professional (I think she got a fiver!) début. And, although it's 'meself as ses it', she was very good. What I liked best on the opening night was when she was supposed to make an exit, and the door stuck. After a couple of pulls and pushes, she just ad libbed and said, 'I think I'll go through the garden – it's quicker,' and exited through the French windows. I thought, 'That's my girl.'

After playing a few Music Halls yet again, I commenced rehearsals for Emile Littler's *Cinderella* at the London Casino. I was to play 'Buttons' with Eve Lister as Prince Charming and Carole Lynne (Lady Delfont) as Cinderella. It was a gorgeous production and again the press was very kind to us, so we settled in for a nice long run. Queen Mary brought Princess Alexandra and Prince Michael of Kent to see a matinée. I was invited to the Royal Box in the interval and the young prince said to me, 'I suppose they call you "Buttons" because you have all those buttons on your uniform?' I felt like saying 'Are you trying to take the mickey?' but refrained. The only members of the cast who did not appear to enjoy playing in the show were the four ponies who pulled Cinderella's coach. They had to walk along a passage from the stage door and be taken down to the stage in the lift. And I was usually in the lift when they arrived! One was a 'biter' and another was a 'kicker' and they certainly didn't like me. One was a bit of a critic too – he passed an opinion all over my costume one night, after which I started to use the stairs. It was either that or my demanding danger money from Emile Littler. Still, it was a great pantomime and, of course, Buttons is my favourite pantomime part. I know I'm too old to play it now, but if they could get Sybil Thorndike to play Cinderella, then I'd have a go!

One night I spotted Stan Laurel in the audience and at the end of the show I made him come up on the stage. This he was very reluctant to do, until I pointed out that he would be mobbed if he didn't. He made a speech, saying it was the first pantomime he'd attended since he saw one at Blackburn in 1910, and he had tears in his eyes and a break in his voice as he reminisced. He was a lovely fellow and sat in my dressing room afterwards until three in the morning just chatting away. I had lunch with him and his wife (I forget which number she was!) the following day, and for years afterwards we kept up a correspondence – he was a compulsive letter writer. My grandchildren now watch old comedies on the television: they love Chaplin, Lloyd and Keaton, even have a chuckle at Gran'pa, but to them Laurel and Hardy are the tops.

After the pantomime had finished, I was soon back in the old routine, playing the Music Halls, which were now very much on the decline. However, I still managed to attract the faithful few, thanks to the radio. Also, at that time, television was beginning to have more impact and I was making the odd appearance to a viewing audience of, I suppose, a few thousand. I spent a little time in Southport with my family. Mother's health had started to deteriorate, but she still followed my every move in show business. The doctor said it was a real tonic to her and he was sure my success had kept her going far more than his medicines could ever have done. The front parlour walls were covered with photographs of me, especially those taken with 'yer Royals'. Mother had a real Victorian admiration and respect for royalty. It was rather like Paul McCartney and his Dad. I was once asked to present Paul with a gold disc and, knowing he must have had dozens presented to him through the years, I asked him what he did with them all. He said he sent them to his father in Liverpool where he had them all displayed round the parlour walls. In the evening, Dad didn't sit and watch the telly, he sat looking at his wonderful son's discs.

A new musical was being prepared for me by Barbara Gordon and Basil Thomas, who had written several of my silly little songs like 'The Pixie', 'The Budgerigar', even 'The Death Watch Beetle'! They had come up with an idea for a show called *The Kid from Stratford*. Briefly the idea was that I dug up an old iron box in my uncle's garden at Stratford-on-Avon, and it contained a musical comedy written by William Shakespeare. In the accompanying letter, Bill said he had written it when he was 'not feeling very well', and had decided that he was no good at writing music. However, he would use the plot as a play which he thought he would call *Hamlet*. It was a very funny script, and with music by Manning Sherwin (and my own faith in my comic ability – big-head!) I felt certain it could be very successful. Jack Hylton was not so sure, so we took it to Jack Waller who had just presented a series of successful Bobby Howes' musicals. He was also the first impresario to import American musicals like *No, No, Nanette* and *Mercenary Mary* in the early twenties. Jack loved the idea of putting me on in what he considered to be a very good vehicle. So in June 1948 we began rehearsals. My leading lady was French this time – Ginette Wander – very petite with a powerful voice, like Edith Piaf, only much prettier. Gil Johnson, the American dancer and singer, played an important part; Jimmy Godden played my father and Chic Elliott, my auntie. Lynette Rae (now Mrs Val Doonican) was the ingénue, and Pauline Grant did the choreography.

As usual, we opened in Manchester at the Palace. The show was about an hour too long on the opening night, but the critics were kind and we knew we had a winner. The two lovers in the show were played by Eunice Gayson and Alfred Marks and, sad to say, they were both wrongly cast. Eunice was very young, very pretty, and had a lovely voice, but at that age she was not a very good actress. Alfred, bald even then and with a glorious bass voice, looked like her father. Even when he was persuaded to wear a toupee, which unfortunately looked like an escalope of veal balanced on his head, it still didn't work. So Eunice and Alfred had to go – one of the sad things that do happen occasionally in the theatre. Their replacements were adequate but never achieved the success that both Eunice and Alfred enjoyed in later years.

We played three weeks in Manchester, then went to Edinburgh for two weeks. Staying at the Caledonian Hotel were Richard Tauber and my old mate Tommy Trinder. They were both appearing in the city, but not in the same show, I hasten to add! A fan brought me a whole salmon one evening so I arranged for the chef at the Caledonian to have it ready for supper after the show. I rang Richard and Tommy and invited them to join me – remember food was still on ration – and we had a real good tuck-in, and lots of laughs. We finished up with me singing 'You are my heart's delight' and Richard giving a rendition of 'The Bee' song, with actions as well.

After Edinburgh, we went to Birmingham, and on the Monday night Jack Hylton and Val Parnell were in front. Jack hated me working for anyone else, so after the show we met at the Queens Hotel, together with Val, and they both tried to persuade me to leave the show. Val said, 'If you open with this rubbish in the West End, they'll tear the seats up and throw them at you!' Charming! But I knew what was behind it all: Jack had bought the rights of an American musical called *High-button Shoes* and wanted me to do it in Val's theatre, the Hippodrome. When we started on tour with *The Kid from Stratford* we were all set to come into the Hippodrome, but Jack Waller only had a verbal contract and he was in tears when he told me they had reneged on their promise. I told him I intended to stick by him and he was able to arrange for us to open at the Princes Theatre, the only West End theatre available.

The Princes was not a fashionable theatre. It was at the wrong end of Shaftesbury Avenue and had a dismal record of flops. However, we opened at the beginning of October to good notices and also good business. As Christmas approached the business began to flag a little, but then we had a stroke of luck. The King and Queen, together with the King and Queen of Denmark, came to see the show one evening. In those days, a visit from royalty was a real accolade to any show, and we were thrilled in the knowledge that it would set the seal of success on our musical.

I was invited to visit the Royal Box in the interval and our King introduced me to the King of Denmark – a very big sailor-type man, tattoos and all, and he shook me very vigorously by the hand. King George said, 'B-b-b-be careful with him. He's only a l-l-l-little fellow.' They said they were all enjoying the show and I asked them if they had to rush away at the end of the show. The King asked why and I said, 'Well, I make a speech at the finale,' and he said, 'Is it funny?' I replied, 'Some people say it's the best part of the show.' The King said, 'All right – we'll stay, but it had better be good.' When I proffered my hand to the King of Denmark, he took the tip of my little finger, just waggled it and said to our King, 'Is that gentle enough?' I made my usual speech at the end of the show and finished up by saying 'You don't half get a cock-eyed view of the show from the box – and I've put on a clean shirt this evening. I think they ought to see it,' and I lay down flat on my back on the stage, facing the box. This received one of the biggest laughs I've ever had on stage.

As Christmas approached, poor Jack Waller received more bad news. Despite the good business we were doing, we had to vacate the theatre because Bert Montagu, the lessee, had arranged to produce his annual Christmas pantomime at the theatre. The only other available theatre for our show was the Winter Gardens in Drury Lane. This was a real white elephant and had been closed for quite some time. But it was cleaned up and we opened up for the Christmas season, with very good bookings. We managed to run until the end of May and then regretfully called it a day. Had *The Kid* been at the Hippodrome as was originally intended, I'm convinced it would have run for two years.

ON 28 SEPTEMBER 1949 my darling mother died. I was appearing at the Kingston Empire, but left for Southport after hearing the news at the end of the show. The management were most considerate and said they would find a deputy for the rest of the week. Mother's death was really a merciful release because she had cancer and had been reduced to almost a skeleton. The *Liverpool Express* summed it all up, saying:

> Mrs Betsy Askey, wife of Mr Samuel Askey and mother of Arthur Askey, the comedian, died at her home in Liverpool Road, Ainsdale, last night after a lengthy illness. A native of Northwich, Mrs Askey was a great lover of the stage and though she never took part in a performance, it was a wish gratified when Arthur chose the stage as a career. Mrs Askey followed Arthur's progress to top rank with great pride.

She was seventy-three when she died, and it gratified me more than I can say when I became well known because I knew what pleasure it gave to her.

Anthea was now making her mark in show business, on radio at any rate. She was playing Violet Elizabeth in the radio version of *Just William* and took part in several of my broadcasts. She also took over a small part in *The Kid from Stratford* towards the end of the run – and very good she was, too. I was now preparing for a trip to Australia and had to make up my mind whether to appear there in *The Love Racket* or *The Kid from Stratford*. Jack Waller was very keen for me to play in the latter as he knew Australia well as an artiste and an impresario. But to Jack Hylton's relief, I decided I would do *The Love Racket* – my judgement told me it was just the show for Down Under. So in November 1949, May, Anthea, and I, together with my secretary (who was to act as company manager), sailed on the *Strathmore*, Australia bound. Roy Royston and Valerie Tandy were the only other members of the original cast and we were joined by Rae Johnson and Audrey Jeans, who were to play the other female leads. What a lovely voyage that was – the best holiday I ever had in my life. We had four and a half weeks in perfect weather in Melbourne, where we were to open.

There were two Indian Rajahs on board – Raj Pipla (whose horse 'Windsor Lad' had won the Derby) and the younger Raj Morvi. They each had their own entourage – chef, doctor, 'minders', etc., and we all became very friendly, so much so that May called Raj Pipla 'Pippy' one evening. I told her quietly that she mustn't be too familiar, so next time they met, she overdid it and called him 'Your Majesty'! Also on board was a very wealthy Parsee family named Bomonji whom I had previously met in London and had supper with at the Savoy, with Jack Buchanan in the party. They were returning to Bombay and the daughter, a most beautiful girl, was completely stage-struck. She organised a ship's concert so that she could perform. Her act consisted of impersonations, the high spot being a take-off of Mae West which frankly was nothing like her.

When we arrived at Bombay we were invited to their home for lunch. We were also invited to cocktails by the two Rajahs at their respective palaces. They were garlanded and carried off the ship by their faithful followers. We joined them for drinks later at their beautiful homes and then we went on to the Bomonjis' for lunch. Their home made the Rajahs' palaces look like Peabody Buildings. It was gorgeous, luxury in excelsis. In the home was a small fully-equipped theatre with seating for about fifty people. This is where the daughter obviously performed to her friends. I christened it 'The Bomonjidrome', much to their amusement.

From Bombay we sailed to Ceylon where we were entertained by Maurice – Dicky Murdoch's brother – who was a tea planter, and he certainly 'showed us a good time'. I had warned the others that Maurice was not a bit like Dicky, he was far more level-headed and sedate. When we left him late that night to return to the ship, he was more like Dicky than Dicky ever was!

We arrived in Melbourne, having called at Perth and Adelaide, where I had been very thoroughly interviewed by both press and radio. A letter was waiting for me at Perth from an Englishman I had never met, welcoming me to Australia and warning me not to criticise anything. He then listed the questions I'd be asked and told me, in all cases, just to say 'Marvellous' with an occasional 'Bloody marvellous'! We rehearsed for two weeks at the Tivoli with the new Australian members of the cast. They were very good, in fact they were 'Marvellous'! We opened to a terrific reception which really thrilled me, and I knew we would run longer than the scheduled six weeks. As a matter of fact, we ran for six months in Melbourne alone. My Australian trip was supposed to be for three months and I stayed for one year. Georgie Wood in *The Performer* in February 1950 wrote, 'Arthur Askey is unquestionably the biggest stage and radio success Australia has ever known – I have this on the best unbiased authority.' We little fellows always stick together! After Melbourne, we had four weeks in Brisbane, four months in Sydney, and the last ten days in Adelaide, so I could watch the English Test Team which had just arrived. I also did a broadcast every Sunday for the ABC, and cannot speak too highly of every aspect of Australian life. The hospitality was killing – they are the most generous people in the world.

Robert Morley was at the other theatre in Melbourne playing in *Edward, my son*. We regularly saw him and his family, including going to tea at their rented house and being entertained by the two kids, Annabelle and Sheridan. They gave us concerts comprising recitations, songs, and dances, at the conclusion of which Robert would spring to his feet and address his wife, May, Anthea, and myself saying: 'Ladies and Gentlemen, my name is Robert Morley. I am a very well-known actor and I can only say this is the finest show I have ever seen. I will now call on Mr Arthur Askey to reply,' and I would have to say something similar while the two kids stood there, lapping it all up. Robert and I were invited to appear in the equivalent of the annual Command Performance, with the Prime Minister and all the heads of the various states in the audience. I had met (Sir) Robert Menzies when he came to see *The Love Racket* at the Tivoli, Melbourne. He came to my dressing room after the show and gave me some wonderful impressions of his colleagues in Parliament, though I didn't know if they were good or bad. I met him several times later, as well as over here in England. I agreed to do the Command; I knew I could do my Music Hall act which they hadn't seen over there. Robert was in a bit of a quandary as to what to perform so I suggested he did a scene from *Edward, my son*. Edward is never seen in the play, so Robert said he would do the scene with the headmaster in which he threatens the headmaster that he will buy the school and sack him if he expels his son. I was then to come on as Edward to give the scene a tag line. So Robert and the actor playing the headmaster did the scene as normal until the point where the master said, 'Would you like to see your son before you go?' In the play, Robert replied, 'No thank you, I don't want to see the young rascal.' However, for this occasion he said, 'Yes – I think I would like to see him.' Then I bounded on, trouser legs rolled up and a school cap on my head, rushed up to Robert and cried, 'Hello, Daddy!' Robert said, 'Edward, my son, I have arranged for you to stay on here for another six years,' to which I replied, 'Another six years in this dump – not bloody likely!' The curtain came down on a big laugh and Robert, the headmaster, and I went in front to take a bow. I stepped forward to make a speech, but explained I was too exhausted after my strenuous part and I'd call on one of the small-part players to respond. Robert stepped forward: 'Ladies and gentlemen. I wrote *Edward, my son* and I have played it all over England and America. Spencer Tracy made a film of it but until tonight nobody – but nobody – had ever seen my son Edward, not even me. But (indicating me) I've always had a horror that he would turn out to look something like this!' So Robert got the last laugh, great performer that he is.

My act went very well – the audience didn't realise I played the piano and hadn't even seen 'The Bee' song in the flesh. At rehearsals

I must admit I was a bit apprehensive. The first turn was two girls called 'Ada and Elsie' who did the Elsie and Doris Waters act verbatim. They were followed by a fellow called 'Whacker' Darve and he did Will Hay's best school sketch. Then came Joey Porter – he did Norman Evans' 'Over the Garden Wall'. And so it went on. I thought somebody was bound to come on and do my act. However, obviously my material hadn't been worth knocking off, so I survived.

I met the Test Team when they arrived in Adelaide – Freddie Brown, Len Hutton, Denis Compton, Cyril Washbrook, and all the lads. It was like a breath of spring. My host at the game was Don Bradman, and to sit in the Pavilion at that glorious ground, with the cathedral and the Blue Mountains beyond, is a breathtaking experience.

When one of the Australian girls in the show left to get married, Anthea took over her part for the rest of the tour and loved appearing in the show. This rather left my little wife very much on her own in a strange land. May was never a good mixer – she had an innate shyness – and she began to fret to get back home. In Sydney we had a flat on Elizabeth Bay overlooking the Harbour and every time she saw an English ship homeward bound, it used to make her very morose. So I knew I must refuse all offers to stay on in the show, or play pantomime, or go on to New Zealand, and get my little missus home.

I received a letter from Emile Littler asking me to play in *Goody Two Shoes* for him at the Casino at Christmas, so I wired back accepting. He sent me a wire confirming, but suggesting I took a cut in the salary he had paid me for *Cinderella*. I wrote back to him saying:

> I am writing this lying in glorious sunshine on Bondi beach. I can stay here indefinitely on my own terms. As I write, I can picture the Casino in Old Compton Street, with the grotty stage door next to the horsemeat shop in Dean Street, and you have the temerity to offer me less money than last time. Count me out!

Emile replied, 'Okay. Same terms as last time. Horsemeat and all.'

We boarded the *Stratheden* (much to May's delight) to return to the old country, and dozens of newly made friends from all over Australia came to see us off, including of course, the Australian members of the cast. I could write a separate book about my stay in Australia – there are so many stories I could tell about a wonderful country and its wonderful people. I have always promised myself another trip out there, but somehow have never got round to it. But perhaps before my band parts go to the British Museum, I will be lucky enough to take another trip Down Under.

We landed at Tilbury on the Sunday and on Monday morning I was at the Casino rehearsing for the pantomime. I had had a good rest on the ship and was raring to go. Anthea was to play Goody Two Shoes. I was the Dame and among others in the cast were Charlie Cairoli and Leon Cortez. Leon played the King and very funny he was too. He was a part-time pig-farmer and one day he asked me if I'd like 'a bit of pork' for the weekend. We were still on rations, so I jumped at the chance. He arrived on the Saturday with a whole pig in a suitcase – I was expecting a couple of chops! Anyway, after the show, I struggled to the stage door with the case and put it down by my car while I went back for another case. When I got back to the car, the case had gone, so somebody else had the 'bit of pork' for the weekend.

We had about a twelve-week run with the pantomime and then it was back to the old routine for me, doing odd weeks at different seaside resorts and Sunday concerts. We had moved into a new flat at Campden Hill, Kensington, so my May was doubly happy to be home. Jack Hylton said he had commissioned Alan Melville to write a new musical for me and I was very excited by this, being a great admirer of Alan's work. He came up with a book in which I was a jockey who dreamed up winners in my sleep. I forecast so many winners that I was kidnapped by some Corsican bandits who wanted to cash in on my predictions. So in the late autumn we started rehearsals for the new opus which was entitled *Bet Your Life*. The cast was marvellous with Julie Wilson, the American girl who had made such a hit in *Kiss Me Kate*, as my wife, and Sally Ann Howes and the late – and very much lamented – Brian Reece playing the other two leading parts.

We opened at the New Theatre, Oxford, just before Christmas and knew we had yet another success on our hands. The (late) Duke

of Marlborough was at the opening night, and he invited Julie, Sally
Ann, and myself to lunch at Blenheim. The two girls were terrible
gigglers and I knew that lunching with the Duke was likely to be
heavy going, so while we were driving to the Palace I warned them
to help with the conversation and try not to giggle. The Duke
greeted us rather remotely, we had a sherry, then went into lunch –
just the four of us, with a butler and a couple of footmen in attendance. As I had anticipated, conversation was not too easy and the
girls (their heads well down over their plates) were less than useless
and trying not to laugh. It was getting a little awkward when suddenly I thought of racing as a subject I knew His Grace was con-
versant with, and proceeded to tell him the story about the man
who won a racehorse in a raffle. This man took the horse to a trainer
and asked him how much he'd want to look after the horse and train
it for him. The trainer said that he wanted fifteen pounds a week,
but the fellow said he couldn't afford it as he only earned twenty
pounds a week. So the trainer said, 'Well, fifteen pounds is my
minimum, but if you go down the lane, there's another trainer
who'll probably be a bit cheaper.' The fellow took his horse to the
next trainer who said he'd do it for ten pounds. The fellow said,
'I still can't afford it as I only earn twenty pounds a week,' so this
trainer said, 'Well, there's a little fellow right down at the end of
the lane. He used to be a very good trainer, till he was warned off
the course – he might do it very cheap for you.' So the fellow walked
his horse down to the decrepit stable at the end of the lane, and this
trainer said he'd look after the horse for thirty bob a week. So the
fellow said, 'Ah, that's better, I can afford that. I'll pay you thirty
bob a week. The only condition is that I must have the manure for
my garden.' The trainer said, 'At thirty bob a week, there ain't going
to be no manure!' The girls, the butler, and the footmen all laughed
discreetly, but the Duke didn't crack a smile. He merely said, after
a long pause, 'Well, of course, pig manure is actually much better
for a garden than horse manure.' That finished the girls – and the
conversation.

From Oxford we went to the Opera House, Manchester, to play
for eight weeks over the Christmas period, and it was a sell-out.
Anthea was in pantomime at nearby Bolton. I asked her to stay with
us at the Midland Hotel, but she wanted to be independent and

stayed with Mrs Wotherspoon ('the best digs in Bolton') with a girlfriend who was in the panto with her. May and I called to see them one very wet morning and Mrs Wotherspoon said they weren't up yet. So we went upstairs to find them sitting up in bed drinking tea with an umbrella over their heads, as the roof was leaking.

We were playing to full houses in Manchester and there was a black market for tickets, but during our last week, the King died. The theatre was closed for the night. We picked up again the following night, but there was a depression on both sides of the footlights. We were due at the London Hippodrome on the following Wednesday, but the opening was postponed until after the King's funeral on the Friday. Then, to my horror, it was announced we would open the following Monday. I knew this would kill the show, as Monday was a bad day in any case, and there was still a feeling of great sadness all around. I pleaded with Jack Hylton and Val Parnell to put our opening back for at least a week, but they were adamant that we started on the Monday. Surprise, surprise, the show went like a bomb, at least the first half did. Early in the second act, Julie and Sally Ann had a great duet called 'All on account of a guy', one of Alan's best lyrics with music by Kenneth Leslie Smith. It stopped the show, as it did in Manchester, and the girls were supposed to repeat the last few bars as an encore. Instead they went right back to the beginning, realised their mistake and – you've guessed it – started to giggle, and lost the audience. We struggled through to the end of the show and then I went forward to make my usual speech and for the first and only time in my life I heard boos from the gallery. I dropped the comicalities and started to talk about our late beloved King and how we all looked forward to having his lovely daughter as our new Queen. This silenced the riff-raff and we got away with it. The Press was very good on the whole: John Barber in the *Daily Express* wrote two notices, one most eulogistic, the other panning the show. The point was that he had to do an early review for the Scottish edition, sending it off at the interval when the show was going so well, then had to write a poor notice when the rot set in during the second act. This incensed Jack Hylton: he had the two notices 'blown up' and displayed outside the Hippodrome under the heading 'Choose Your Barber'! Anyway, we got a nine-month run out of the show. Julie Wilson left the cast, as she had commitments in America, and Noel Gordon took her place. I used to make my appearance in the finale on horse-back, dressed as a jockey. The horse was a beautiful animal called 'Marquis'. He had come down from Manchester to be with us in London, and he only disgraced himself once during the whole run. Not like the horse in *Gone with the Wind* at Drury Lane, who did it centre stage on the opening night. Also in the show was a terrible, precocious little girl who got on everybody's nerves, and when Noël Coward (who was in the audience on the first night) was asked what he thought of the show he said, 'If only they had stuck that terrible child up the horse's arse, it would have been much better!'

I love horses, but strangely enough, one of my pet hates (and I have many!) is horse racing. I loathe owners, trainers, jockeys, bookies, commentators, punters, betting shops – anything at all to do with racing, except the horses themselves. Having seen the Grand National, it was always my ambition to throw a saddle over Mrs Mirabelle Topham and ride her over the appalling Aintree fences. I think that racing attracts the layabouts from every strata of society and if I were a dictator, I would stop racing of every kind. There is only one motive for the racegoer, and that is how to make money without working for it. To my way of thinking, most of Social Security goes on the horses, as well as a lot of wage packets. People often ask me – Pete Murray on his radio show, for instance – why I have this loathing. It may be that I'm a frustrated jockey or that I have known great performers like Eddie Gray and Jimmy James who gave all their hard-earned wages to non-tax-paying bookies. Bud Flanagan was the wise one: when he found he couldn't beat them, he joined them! They don't get a bob out of me, not even for the Derby or the Grand National. Vote for Askey – and down with racing!

But I do like watching football and cricket, even though those two pastimes are now being spoiled by the hooligans who are now part of our society. As a member of the M.C.C., Middlesex and the Lords' Taverners, I used to love to go to Lords and sit in the sun watching a game of cricket and having a doze when it became bogged down. But not any longer. The shouting, jeering, blowing whistles, and running on the pitch has taken all the charm away and

Presenting Gold Disc to Paul and Linda McCartney.

Opposite page, Top: This is your life. *Bottom:* Fifty years in show biz with Danny La Rue, Roger Moore, Jimmy Edwards, Eric Morecambe and Ernie Wise.

Below: With Prince Charles and Eric Morecambe at the 'Goon Show Scripts' launching

Left to Right: Anthea, Andrew, me, Bill, Jane, William Arthur

I haven't watched a live cricket match for the past five or six years. And how different the crowds are at football matches these days, compared with only a few years ago. Tom Whitaker, then the Arsenal manager, rang me during the run of *Bet Your Life* and asked me if I would go to Highbury and help entertain the crowds at a cup-tie they were having against Spurs. The gates were to be opened at eleven o'clock and although they had a military band, the Dagenham Girl Pipers, and some athletic stunts, Tom felt a few 'ighly comical remarks from the commentary box would help to pass the time till kick-off. I was only too happy (it meant I got in free!) and told him I would bring (the late) Jack Train (Colonel Chinstrap of ITMA) along with me. After each stint on the pitch by the band or the athletics, Jack and I would crack a few gags over the loud-speakers, usually something like 'Here are the team changes – goal, Stafford Cripps, full backs, Rita Hayworth and Aly Khan, half backs, Freeman Hardy & Willis,' etc., and such assorted pleasan-tries. Just before the game commenced, Jack and I went into the players' dressing room and I donned Leslie Compton's tracksuit (he was well over six feet) and Jack put on an equally large one. We found a rugby ball (which happened to be there for some unknown reason) and went out on to the pitch, to enormous cheers. I tipped the police off to chase us off and give us the 'bums' rush' when Jack kicked the ball over the bar, as we had planned. As we walked to the centre of the field, Jack put his foot out and tripped me up. I pulled a whistle out of my pocket, blew it, and pointed to the penalty spot. I took up my position in goal, Jack placed the rugby ball on the penalty spot, the idea being he ballooned it miles over the bar. Instead of which he scored the best goal of the afternoon! The police rushed on and I gave them a real run for their money. Poor Jack, never too athletic with his wheezy chest, was easily caught and when I was finally led down the players' tunnel, I found him being attended to by the ambulance men. Anyway, he soon recovered and we sat and enjoyed the game, with no yobs running on the pitch and no broken shop windows or smashed-up tube trains after the game.

Bet Your Life having finished its run, I was engaged by Prince Littler for his *Babes in the Wood* pantomime at the Brighton Hippo-drome, filling in the intervening time with Music Hall dates, Sunday concerts, radio, and now increasingly television programmes. In 1952 more and more people were buying sets and what had been looked on as a one-day wonder was now becoming a real menace to every other branch of the entertainment industry.

FOR MANY YEARS, I had given up my Christmas night at home
to take part in 'The BBC Christmas Party' on radio, and now the
same thing was happening on television. A host of 'stars' were all
supposed to be (self-consciously) enjoying themselves for the amusement of listeners or viewers who were ostensibly full of Christmas
good cheer and would not notice how contrived it all was. At the
1952 party, one of the comedians engaged to take part was so full
of good cheer himself that he couldn't do his act. You can ask
Terry-Thomas – he was there! Ronnie Waldman, then director of
television Light Entertainment, asked me if I could fill in the necessary six or eight minutes, so I just messed about with 'funny walks'
and chatted to the camera ('Count my freckles,' etc.) and found I
had made quite a hit. So much so that Ronnie said he wanted me
to do a series when the pantomime finished. I had anticipated this –
I thought he'd never ask! I registered the title with him there and
then: *Before Your Very Eyes*.

With the help of marvellous scripts by Sid Colin and Talbot
Rothwell (writer of the *Carry On* films) and the support of Dickie
Henderson and Diana Decker, the first television comedy series in

front of a studio audience was launched in March 1953. It was *Band Waggon* all over again. The critics said I was the only comedian who knew how to use the camera – I made it my friend instead of being afraid of it. The half-hour was made up of three sketches (after an introduction) and I would have to change from, say, Florence Nightingale to Sherlock Holmes, then to Rupert of Hentzau while some other character or characters did half a page of dialogue. It was all a big lark in those days and if I felt like walking off the set ('Isn't it funny where this room ends,' or, in a Foreign Legion sketch, 'Fancy the desert finishing here!') then the camera had to follow me. There was no cutting to cameras 2, 3, or 4. There was no tape recording, and the show was very much 'live', and all the better for it. Many's the time I've rushed on half-dressed to ask them to talk slower or 'Would you mind saying that all over again!' As with the Morecambe and Wise show today, all the top actors, announcers, and musicians were dying to appear on the show. There were new series in 1955, 1956, and 1957. Unfortunately Dickie Henderson could not appear in these and therefore I felt I wanted to give the show a gimmick of some sort. So I hit on the idea of having a dumb blonde around the set. The BBC was rather alarmed and wanted to know what I intended to do with her! I didn't know myself at the time, but I got my own way, and so Sabrina was born. We held auditions for a suitable dumb-cluck and found one in Norma Sykes. She had a lovely face and figure, but could not act, sing, dance, or even walk properly, although she had come to London to try her luck as a model. I asked her what she was doing and she told me she was making artificial jewellery, as her broken nails bore witness. Anyway, she was exactly what we wanted.

I had just finished appearing in a farce at the Palace Theatre and this was followed by a show called *Sabrina Fair*, so I changed her name from Norma to Sabrina. You will have to take my word that I did not engage her on the size of her bust. I knew she was 'well built' but had no idea how big she really was until the BBC wardrobe mistress told me she couldn't get Sabrina into a medieval costume on account of her enormous chest. I realised then that I had unknowingly struck 'gold in them thar hills'! But she really was 'dumb' in those days. I was opening a garden fête and was asked if I would bring her along. After the opening the vicar's young daughter curtsied and presented Sabrina with a bouquet of flowers. 'Sabby' said, 'No thank you – we've got plenty of flowers at home'! She eventually became bigger (in every sense) than me in the show and we couldn't keep the Fleet Street reporters and interviewers away from Lime Grove. The tail began to wag the dog, so she had to go. But with the money she made she had acting, singing, dancing, and deportment lessons and eventually finished up doing a very polished cabaret act with special songs, usually about her deformity! People often ask me 'Whatever happened to Sabrina?' and I tell them that she is now married to an American doctor and living in Hollywood. Whenever she visits this country, she usually calls on me, and she looks a million dollars, with her American grooming and her mid-Atlantic accent. Who said I wasn't a talent-spotter!

Those were exciting days in television, but I don't suppose there were more than one-and-a-half million viewers at that time. As usual I was a pioneer and did all my best work then, or before people knew any better. When commercial television came along, I was immediately offered more money to join them by Jack Hylton, who was a shareholder. So my next four series between 1957 and 1961 were all seen on the rival channel. They were all right, but did not have anything like the quality of the BBC shows – after all, commercial TV was in a very dicey position at the outset, and everything was skimped. Dickie Murdoch and I tried to put *Band Waggon* on the TV screen in a series entitled *Living It Up*. Ostensibly we lived in a flat on the roof of Associated Rediffusion in Kingsway, but it just didn't work out. On radio people had their own idea of what our flat looked like and you couldn't transfer it to the television screen.

I returned to the BBC for another series in 1961. It was called *Raise Your Glasses* and was written by Alan Melville, who also took part. It was not a world-shattering success, but we enjoyed doing it. Alan is great to work with and a marvellous writer. The head of BBC Light Entertainment at that time was Tom Sloan. Alan was not one of his admirers and if you read Alan's biography *Merely Melville*, pages one and two, you will see why.

Jack Hylton had booked me to play in a farce at the Grand Theatre, Blackpool, for the summer season of 1953. We had not settled on a vehicle, but while I was in panto at Brighton, I saw a comedy at the Dolphin Theatre called *Just My Bill* with Thora Hird, Leo Franklyn, Danny Ross, and the author Glenn Melvyn in the cast. It was very funny indeed, so I phoned Jack Hylton and suggested he had a look at it. He came down with Richard Bird, the director, and saw at once that this was just the job for Blackpool. The play had had a short run in small theatres and was about to be taken off, so Glenn was delighted when Jack said he wanted it for Blackpool. There was a fair amount of love interest and political reference in the script which I soon deleted at rehearsals, and the play was rechristened *The Love Match*. Hylton liked the word 'love' in his titles.

After a week's 'breaking it in' at the New Theatre, Oxford, we opened at Blackpool with great success. With Thora, Danny, Glenn, and my daughter, Anthea, it turned out to be a riot of corny fun – just what the holidaymakers wanted.

Jack Hylton had one of his hunches and thought *The Love Match* would do well in the West End, so he booked the Palace Theatre for October. Like everyone else, I thought he was mad. A little north country, seven-handed farce in that big West End theatre, and playing twice nightly, was against all theatrical tradition. With his usual charm, Jack persuaded me to fall in with the idea, so when we'd finished at Blackpool, we went to the Palace, Manchester, for two weeks' capacity business, then on to London. The show went like a bomb and all the critics accepted it for what it was and gave us very good notices. Just one exception: the critic who said Jack Hylton had brought the show to town 'because it appealed to the millions who saw a televised excerpt'. He went on, '. . . which suggests dismaying possibilities. If West End productions are to be selected according to TV standards of light entertainment, the end of the theatre will be in sight.' The critic in question was that failed actor, Kenneth Tynan ('Shakespeare with a stutter'), who later gave us such cultural masterpieces as *Oh! Calcutta!*

After six months at the Palace, we transferred to the Victoria Palace where The Crazy Gang had just finished a long run. Hylton still had the lease of the theatre, so he saved paying rent on the transfer. John Baxter, the film producer, wanted to make a picture of *The Love Match* at the Beaconsfield studios. I was keen to make another film but not while the show was still playing. So Lupino

Lane went into the Victoria Palace and played my part for seven weeks while I revelled in the break from playing the theatre twice nightly.

It was a very hot August and I met several of my theatrical friends who said they were going on, or were just coming back from, location filming in Switzerland, Africa, the south of France, Norway, etc. I said airily, 'Oh, I'm going on location with my picture next week.' They were very intrigued and asked me where. I told 'em: 'The railway yards at Bolton,' and, 'We have pies and peas in the canteen there too.' The picture, made on a small budget naturally, showed a huge profit, doing marvellous business everywhere. I was on a salary so didn't make out as well as Hylton and his associates. However, it got me back into pictures and I followed it up by making *Ramsbottom Rides Again*, in which I had a small percentage interest. Then another film came up, based on my own idea of a make-up man at the BBC being bribed to put out commercials during the BBC programmes. The country was fascinated by the commercials shown on ITV at this time, so it was quite a novelty. I insisted I had an interest in this picture and put money into the production. It was the only film I ever made which lost money! I have seen it twice on TV and every 'frame' in the hour and a half was like a knife stab! I made one more picture after that – *Friends and Neighbours* – but on salary this time! I was never made to be a Sam Goldwyn!

Came 1954 and Anthea's twenty-first birthday. (She'll kill me for quoting dates!) The birthday itself was celebrated backstage at the Palace Theatre with a cake and a bottle of cooking sherry. The big shindig took place at the Dorchester with 150 guests the following Sunday. Anthea was allowed to invite one or two of her friends, but the majority of the guests were, I'm afraid, 'show biz'. Flanagan and Allen, Nervo and Knox, Naughton and Gold, Eddie Gray, Norman Wisdom, Dickie Murdoch, Julie Wilson, Sally Ann and Bobby Howes, Jack Hylton, Brian Reece – you name them, they were all there! Anthea at that time had a crush on Herbert Lom who was appearing in *The King and I* at Drury Lane, so I secretly invited him and when he turned up it made Anthea's night.

I asked all the pros to do the acts they were performing when they were twenty-one and this provided a marvellous cabaret. The star

was undoubtedly Jimmy Nervo. He had been an acrobat, so he took
off his dinner jacket, went out of the ballroom and came rushing
across the dance floor doing the most sensational back flips at in-
credible speed before disappearing through the opposite door. He
came back puffing and panting to tremendous cheers which turned
into terrific laughter when the real acrobat he had hired came on to
take a call! Anyway, Anthea's twenty-first was a night to remember,
and although Herbert Lom's presence there pleased her, she was
even more pleased to have the stage manager of *The Love Match* as
a guest. This was Bill Stewart, who was later to become her husband.

March 1954 saw the closing down of Alexandra Palace as a television studio. I was asked to take part in the wake and had to rush
from the Palace Theatre as soon as the curtain came down in order
to get there. When I arrived, everybody was well and truly plas-
tered. As one critic said, 'The show dragged its way wearily along
for more than three-and-a-half hours with the result that at times
it became nostalgic! It only brightened up at the end when Arthur
Askey came on.' So in addition to all the Music Halls I'd closed, I
could now add the Alexandra Palace to the list!

The Love Match finished its run and I was now free for the
summer. I signed with Harold Fielding to take part in his 'Music
for the Millions' shows. These took place at Bournemouth, Eastbourne, Folkestone, Llandudno, etc., and were 'classy' entertainment, a cut above the ordinary seaside shows. They were labelled
'cultural' and were, in consequence, exempt from paying entertainment tax. However, the Commissioners of Customs and Excise
moved in and a 'perfectly friendly action' took place between them
and the Eastbourne Corporation. The result was hilarious – legal
imbecilities at their best. Peter Brough, the ventriloquist, was involved and the learned counsel was asked about Archie Andrews,
his dummy. Counsel replied, 'Archie Andrews, I understand, is not
a person at all, although he was once assessed for income tax. He is,
I understand, a piece of wood or material.' The Entertainments
Manager, Mr Hill, was asked 'Did Mr Arthur Askey make remarks
about his combinations?' 'I can't remember,' said Mr Hill, proving
what an impact I had made on him. Sir Reginald Manningham-
Buller, Q.C., then asked Mr Hill about two jokes concerning seaside
landladies I had used, and repeated them. 'I knocked at the door,

the landlady opened it. I asked if she could put me up and she said "I'll want ten pounds a week and I don't want any children." She asked me if I would mind making my own bed and I said "No" so she gave me a hammer and some nails and a few pieces of wood.' To hear these gags told in the solemn surroundings of the Court, with Mr Justice Danckwerts and Mr Millward Tucker as well as Sir Reginald in attendance, was hilarious. What the outcome of the case was I never heard, but it would have made wonderful material for dear old Robb Wilton in his Mr Muddlecombe series on radio.

I enjoyed doing the shows for Harold. With my old friend Sydney Jerome to play golf with (and accompany me on the piano as a sideline) we'd travel in his car or mine from one seaside town to another, often doing a Sunday concert on the way. I nearly killed him on the golf course at Llandudno. He was pointing the direction I should drive to a 'blind' hole and I did a terrific slice and caught Syd right in the midriff. He doubled up like a closing jack-knife and it took a long time to pull him round. On his tummy he had the word 'Dunlop' clearly imprinted for days and as he was a bit on the plump side, I must say it suited him!

My next major chore was pantomime at the Golders Green Hippodrome for jolly Jack Hylton. I was back in my drawers playing 'Big-hearted Martha' the children's nurse, in *Babes in the Wood*. Sally Ann Howes was Robin Hood, and a very happy pantomime it was. In all, I did four pantomimes at Golders Green and among our regular customers were Harold Wilson and his family and Sir Donald Wolfit and his wife. I had met Sir Donald at a charity concert held at the Scala Theatre. I was compèring the show with Tommy Trinder – he announced one artiste and I would announce the next. Sir Donald was very nervous and pacing up and down in the wings muttering his lines. He was going to recite 'Fagin's last night alive'. Semprini was playing the piano and Sir Donald called me over to him and said, 'I follow this, don't I?' I told him he did, so he said to me (knowing it was Tommy's turn to do the announcing) 'Well, I don't want to be introduced by a comedian – will you do it?'!

Madame Tussauds approached me to be 'done in wax'. They had asked me previously in 1939, but the war put the kibosh on it at that time. I went along and my vital statistics were duly noted. They

put my hands in wax to make a cast of them and I yelled when they
pulled it off – I had more hairs on my hands than I thought. They
asked me to let them have a suit and they would supply me with a
new one. They explained that a suit that had been worn hung better
on the figure, even the trousers, which depended on which side the
male 'dressed'! They put a blob of wax up in the crotch, either on
the left side or the right. Confidentially they told me they had only
ever had one subject who dressed on the right, and that was a duke.
Anyway, whoever heard of a duke with leanings towards the left!
They told me other interesting bits of quaint happenings in Tussauds. For instance, about the nightwatchman who fell for Lady
Jane Grey and how they found evidence that he made love to her
most nights. The launching of my wax figure was done in front of
the television cameras and made a very good hour's entertainment,
I thought. I said that Tussauds had opened 150 years ago with just
one figure, Vic Oliver (dear old Vic), and when they showed the
girls sticking single hairs into my (wax) head I said, 'I must tell
David Nixon about this.' The show finished with me apparently
lost and locked up in the Chamber of Horrors. As we hadn't started
the programme until after ten o'clock when the customers had gone,
it was well past midnight by the time I got downstairs among
Crippen and Co. The latest addition was Christie's kitchen where
he buried the bodies, and as I sat in the bath in which Smith
drowned three of his wives, I must confess I felt a little nervous.

The next time I saw my figure in Tussauds was when I went to
do a *Candid Camera*. They removed my figure and I stood 'live'
amongst the models of Peter Sellers, Harry Secombe, Terry-
Thomas, etc., right up at the front (we're back to Sabrina again!).
It was about 11 a.m. and there were very few customers at that hour.
However, a young fellow and his girl came round, stood in front of
me, looked at their programme and said, 'Oh, there's so and so –
there's so and so – oh – and here's Arthur Askey.' At that, I did a
most terrific sneeze, and the girl went spark out on the floor. We had
a little conference and decided the stunt was too risky. If that had
been a woman with a heart complaint, she might have died. So then
I stood with my hands on the back of a bentwood chair and when
people came along, Jonathan Routh distracted them for a minute
by pointing to the figures on the other side of the corridor. When

they turned back to me, I had sat down on the chair. The puzzlement on their faces had to be seen to be believed.

The last time I saw myself at Tussauds, I had been 'sawn in half' and was sitting behind a table with David Jacobs on 'Juke Box Jury'. I've probably been melted down by now and reworked to appear as Raquel Welch. Though of course for Miss Welch they would have to add two extra blobs of wax, instead of the one they used for me!

In 1956 I decided I would take a holiday in the south of France. All my rich friends assured me there was no place like it, so May and I flew to Nice, then travelled to Juan-les-Pins, which we came to adore and spent the next ten years' holidaying there. We went early in the season before the crowds arrived, and on our first evening there we sat in the little square, drinking coffee and enjoying the tranquillity of the place. How lovely to get away from it all and show biz in particular. Within the next half-hour we had been joined by Dickie Henderson, Norman Wisdom, Jimmy Jewel and Ben Warriss, all with their wives and, like us, getting away from it all. We were later joined by Alan Melville, so all thoughts of an early night went by the board. But we had some wonderful holidays in Juan, meeting up with (Sir) Lew Grade and Kathy, and also Prince and Emile Littler, who had villas at Antibes and Cannes respectively, and of course, Jack Hylton, who also had two houses at Antibes. But May and I spent quite a lot of time just enjoying each other's company, lying on the beach all day (where we also had lunch) and finding somewhere pleasant to eat in the evening. We usually went into the Casino each night, not to gamble but for May to have a pot of tea while I had a beer. C'est la vie! But for me, the Côte d'Azur is the only place for a holiday.

I was back to the British seaside resorts on my return – Aberdeen, Llandudno, Margate, Bournemouth, Torquay, Yarmouth, Skegness, etc. The travelling was more tiring than the actual work and I resolved I would take a resident summer season the following year. May travelled with me for most of the time and we were glad to get back to our flat in town for the autumn. May used to like tea at Fortnum and Mason, so I arranged to meet her there one afternoon the first week we were back. I arrived at the tea lounge and the supervisor said, 'Mrs Askey has arrived,' and took me past all the tables occupied by tea-drinking ladies, to where May was sitting.

When I sat down, all faces in the restaurant were looking at me and I heard the whispers 'There's Arthur Askey' as I was being ushered in. As I've said before it's hell to be the rage! May said to me, 'Look who's at the next table,' and it was Charlie Chaplin with another man. Chaplin saw all the eyes looking in our direction and I heard him say to his friend, 'I've been spotted. Let's get the bill and get out.' I didn't like to lean over and say, 'It's not you, cock, it's me they're looking at,' as he, of course, didn't know me from Adam. The waitress came over, said how she loved me on the telly and the radio and would I sign her book and she took no notice of Charlie, who was vainly trying to attract her attention to get his bill. He said to his friend, 'How *do* you get a bill here?' so I butted in and said, 'Just get up and walk out, you'll have your bill before you're twenty yards up Piccadilly.' He laughed and said, 'The two hardest things to get in a restaurant are a bill and a glass of water.' He then asked me if I knew if there was a bus from Piccadilly to Lancaster Gate. I said, 'I couldn't tell you, I'm very rich and travel everywhere by car.' He said he used to deliver bottles of medicine for a doctor in Lancaster Gate (he was paid a penny for each bottle delivered) and wanted to see if the house was still standing. Anyway, he eventually got the bill, and walked out unrecognised by the customers, not realising he had been talking to one of the all-time greats!

I have been around for a long time and almost take it for granted when I am recognised. I did meet a Waterloo a few months ago when I attended a midday function in the City, where Mr Enoch Powell was to unveil a cartoon which was to be used as a pub sign. I had been one of the panel of selectors who had to judge the winner from about two dozen cartoons which had been submitted. Mr Powell arrived in his raincoat and black homburg and the organiser said he would look after them for him. But Mr Powell is no fool – when that happens you don't know where your hat and coat are if and when you want to make a quick exit. So he said he would put them somewhere convenient: 'How about behind this curtain?' which he pulled aside and disclosed the masterpiece he was about to unveil! Afterwards in the V.I.P. room he seemed to notice I was getting as much attention as he was and he said to me, 'What do you do?' I thought he was kidding, but wasn't too sure, so I said, 'Oh, I'm a comical codger who tries to make people laugh.' He asked, 'What are you doing now?' so I told him I was rehearsing for pantomime at Richmond. He said, 'I love pantomime – can I come and see it?' I said I would try and arrange it and he warned me he would also like to bring his wife and two daughters. I told the management and they evidently contacted him because soon afterwards I received a letter on House of Commons notepaper which read:

Dear Mr Askey,
Thank you for remembering the generous suggestion which you made when we met at the Cartoonist. I am extremely disappointed that I have to fly to Australia on 30th December and so shall miss the performance, but it will be enjoyed by my family, who assure me that I shall never live down the shame of failing to recognise one so much more famous than myself.
(My wife, having heard me dictate these words, ejaculated 'I should think not indeed!')
With all good wishes,
Yours sincerely,
J. Enoch Powell

I wrote back to him and said that I had heard many excuses for not having to sit through a pantomime, but going all the way to Australia was ridiculous!

One of the funniest experiences I had of being – or not being – recognised was when I was staying at a hotel in Eastbourne where I was appearing in a summer show two years ago. I was coming down in the lift and a man got in at the floor below, looked at me and said:

Man: 'Arthur!'
Me: 'Yes.'
Man: 'I'll bet everybody calls you that.'
Me: 'Yes, they do.'
Man: 'Well you are like him you know. Mind you, he's getting on a bit now – I think he must be seventy.'
Me: 'I think he's older than that – about seventy-two.'

Man: 'Is he? He wears well, doesn't he?'
Me: 'He certainly does.'

With that, we both got out of the lift and that was that. However, the following day the same thing happened – he again got in the lift and said 'Arthur'. I thought well, he knows who I am now until he said, 'Here, I hear he was in the hotel yesterday, pity we didn't see him.' Then there were the two ladies at Blackpool: one spotted me and said to her friend, 'Ee – there's Arthur Askey.' The other one had a good look at me, and said, 'He's just like he looks, isn't he!'

Anthea became Mrs Bill Stewart on her birthday in 1956. The ceremony took place at All Souls, Langham Place, with movie and TV cameras, press photographers and crowds of people on the pavements and in the hotel and office windows opposite. Anthea is like me, always miles too early for any appointment, and we had to drive around for about twenty minutes before arriving at the church. The reception was at the Savoy and, like her twenty-first birthday, was a real show biz shindig. I had had my share of the champagne and when I made my speech, I referred to all the comedians who were there. I said, 'If a bomb was to fall on this place, so and so (mentioning a comic who wasn't there) would come into his own!' This was duly reported in the Press the following day. You can imagine the atmosphere when this particular comic and I were in the same pantomime a couple of years later. Anyway, the wedding was a big success, and so was the bill!

Anthea did not give up the business. She played the title role with me in *Humpty Dumpty* at the Golders Green Hippodrome that Christmas, then went on to do two or three very successful TV series with Dickie Henderson, until she became pregnant in 1959. After the pantomime had finished I did my usual 'fill-ins' with radio, TV and odd shows, and then set about fixing the summer season I had promised myself. To my amazement, I found the managements were not falling over themselves for my services. But I was quite philosophical about it – I was now fifty-seven and had had a long and successful run, so had to accept things. Anyway, I arranged to go to Rhyl for the season. I was quite happy to do this, as Rhyl and 'The Jovial Jesters' had been partly responsible for me being in show biz. But Rhyl was not in the 'big league' of seaside resorts such as Blackpool, Yarmouth, Torquay, Bournemouth, etc., so I naturally felt I had dropped into the second division. We had a very good show all the same, with my old mate Jerry Desmonde acting as my 'feed'.

One day the phone rang and it was Val Parnell: would I star in the Palladium pantomime next Christmas? You can imagine my feelings – I felt 'wanted' again. And Ches Allen, my agent, fixed the details and got me a thousand pounds a week for the first two weeks of the run. My salary dropped considerably after that, but at least I could tell all and sundry I was getting four figures – for the only time in my life. But it was the morale booster that counted most.

THE SUBJECT of the Palladium pantomime was *Robinson Crusoe* –
I was to play Mrs Crusoe and my two sons were Robinson and
Billy. Robinson was to be played by David Whitfield, then the most
popular singer in the country, and Billy was none other than Tommy
Cooper. There's a character.

The interval scene was an underwater ballet, the ship, captained
by Robinson Crusoe, having been sunk. It was a beautiful scene –
Robert Nesbit at his best – and the girls, some of them on wires,
were all around the stage doing balletic movements. From the
centre, the lift rose with a huge sea shell as its centrepiece. The shell
opened and I stepped out in my tutu and blonde wig and did a bit
of cod ballet. I suggested to Bob Nesbit that it would be an effective
and funny ending if Tommy Cooper came down from the flies on
a wire, dressed as a skin diver – snorkel, oxygen cylinder, flippers
and all – and rescued me. We all thought it a funny idea and had,
of course, to explain it to Tommy very slowly. Came the rehearsal,
I did my bit of ballet and waited for my rescuer's arrival. Above the
noise of the orchestra (and the laughter from the girls) I could hear
shouts of pain coming from Tommy. As I mentioned before, a

leather flying harness is not the most comfortable of garments, especially for a man. I took Tommy on one side and told him the secret was to pad yourself between the legs with a couple of towels. So we tried it once more, again to howls of anguish from Tommy. (He's a big boy, remember.) I told him to put even more padding 'underneath the arches', and now it was time for the actual first-night show. All went well until I came out of my shell, did my dance, then waited for Sir Galahad. I looked up – no sign of him. Suddenly I heard the sound of flippers behind me and he just flapped across the stage, took my arm and led me off to the wings. I started to protest, but he said, 'I'm not standing for that coming down on a wire lark – I'm too fond of children!'

During the run of the pantomime, I developed a bit of voice trouble – unusual for me, with my lungs of brass. I have always prided myself that I could be heard at the back of the gallery, without the aid of a microphone. Anyway, I went to see a throat specialist in Wimpole Street and he told me I had acute laryngitis and must rest my voice for at least a week. So I stayed off the show for the Friday and Saturday (which with the Sunday gave me three days rest) but by the Monday, I was back for the matinée. I got through the next five weeks to the end of the pantomime, and then immediately made a long-playing record, followed by another TV series, but my voice was far from normal. On the sixth (and last) of the programmes, my voice gave out completely at dress rehearsal and one of my earlier shows was transmitted that night. One throat specialist said I had to rest my voice, another said I must try and force it up, but they both agreed I was badly in need of a rest.

I had some cards printed which said 'Transmission temporarily suspended' which I handed to anyone who spoke to me. I couldn't even whisper. May and I took off for the south of France and I just lazed about in the sun for three weeks. But there was no sign of my voice reappearing. May phoned the specialist and he said I was to return to London at once. The following day I entered University College Hospital for all kinds of tests, including that charming caper where they stick a long tube down the throat and have an exploration around the stomach. Everything seemed to be normal, so they packed me off again to the south of France for more rest and relaxation. I was met at Nice airport by May, Lew and Kathy Grade, Jimmy and Belle Jewel, Dickie Henderson and all the gang carrying placards with comic messages. But there was anxiety all round and the welcome back meal was on the quiet side, especially as I had to write down all that had happened. After two weeks I returned to London and on the advice of the specialist I went to a speech therapist, but it was hopeless. There was no sign of any improvement.

I recalled a singing coach who had attended Sally Ann Howes, Julie Wilson, the late David Hughes and others when they had suffered with voice trouble. He had even coached Laurence Olivier to sing in *The Beggar's Opera*. His name was Georges Cunelli, known as 'The Maestro', and frankly I had thought of him as a bit of a charlatan when he was brought up time and again from London to Manchester to attend artistes with vocal problems. With great patience and care, he began to coax my voice back, and to say that I was eternally grateful to him would be an understatement. He was just as thrilled, and kept saying that I had as good a voice as David Hughes and one day I would sing 'Plaisir d'amour' and astonish everybody. I told him I wasn't that ambitious and was quite content just to be able to talk again and sing 'The Bee' song.

It was grand being able to get back to work again and the only sad note was that my Dad died at the age of eighty-three, still wondering if I had done the right thing by giving up my job at the Education Offices. My sister Rene moved down to London and the last of the Askeys had now left Merseyside.

In the autumn, I was very busy with television, which was now becoming more and more popular. One successful programme was *This Is Your Life*, which I thought was an embarrassing show and swore they'd never catch me for. But they did. I was coming out of a TV rehearsal (for the commercial channel) with Brian Tessler and MacDonald Hobley when we noticed a BBC van at the bottom of the steps. Mac Hobley said, 'What's a BBC van doing here?' Then out stepped Eamonn Andrews with the book and the well-known death knell: 'Arthur Askey – this is your life.' I was then bundled into a car and on the way to Shepherds Bush I tried to put up a mild resistance, but Eamonn said, 'Don't let us down, we've got all sorts of relatives and friends there and a packed audience in the studio.' I said, 'Well, one relative you won't have there is my little wife,' but he said, 'You're wrong, she's there all right.' Which just shows Eamonn's powers of persuasion, for if anyone ever shunned the limelight, it was my May. The programme followed its usual pattern and I reacted with great surprise as each old acquaintance or relative was introduced. I had to over-act when one fellow from Liverpool 'who had been my best friend' came on and I had, and still have, no idea who he was! Anthea appeared on film as she was very pregnant, as did Dickie Murdoch (not pregnant, I hasten to add). May surprised me with the ease and humour she displayed, and Rene came on at the end dressed like me. Poor girl, she's so like me, she has to stay indoors when I'm playing Dame in pantomime!

I would not put my *This Is Your Life* show among the top twenty. But sixteen years later . . . It is now December 1974. I am asked to do a TV discussion show, talking about pantomime with Ted Ray and Jimmy Tarbuck. We are surrounded by pantomime animals – the cow, the cat, etc. – and the fairy, when suddenly 'Humpty Dumpty' waddles on and throws back the top of the egg. Out pops Eamonn, book in hand, and says (giving an impression of Mike Yarwood), 'Arthur Askey – for the *second* time, this is your life.' (That's another record broken – I'm the only one old enough to be 'done' twice.) What a star-studded cast I had this time: darling Gracie Fields who had flown in from Capri, Sabrina who had travelled from Hollywood, Val Doonican, Jack Warner, June Whitfield, Dickie Henderson, David Nixon, Kathleen Harrison, Norman Vaughan, Jimmy Jewel, MacDonald Hobley, Barbara Mullen, Cyril Fletcher, Charlie Drake, Peter Butterworth, Jimmy Logan, and Charlie Chester! Dickie Murdoch was again in South Africa so had to appear on film, as did Ken Dodd, who spoke from a classroom at the Liverpool Institute. They also unearthed one of my old colleagues from the Education Offices – Frank Ball, now happily retired, as I would have been had I followed Father's advice. And, of course, Anthea appeared with Bill, her husband, and my three darling grandchildren – and, naturally, my sister Rene. All in all, it was a marvellous thrill for me, only marred by the fact that I could not stay for the orgy afterwards as I had to appear in cabaret at Bournemouth at 11 o'clock.

Another very popular TV show at the time of my first *This Is Your Life* was *What's My Line?*, in which I took part both on the panel (where I was useless – it was too 'polite' for me) and as the mystery guest. I did this twice and was easily spotted the first time, so on the second occasion I went to the wardrobe, got a lady's dress that rustled, and sprinkled some of the producer's secretary's perfume on it. When I was asked to 'sign in', I held the frock to me and minced past the blindfolded panel before sitting down by Eamonn Andrews. Gilbert Harding started the questioning by saying, 'Well our guest is obviously a lady,' which got a good laugh from the audience. He looked puzzled and said, 'Tell me, madam,' which again got a big laugh. Gilbert now started to lose his cool and every question he asked was greeted by a roar of laughter. When I was finally rumbled by David Nixon and the panel removed their masks, Gilbert's anger knew no bounds and he had a real tantrum about how unfair it was. I calmed him down, pointing out that it was only a game and played for light entertainment, but he was very truculent for the rest of the show. In the hospitality room afterwards he apologised to me for getting so ratty. Beneath it all, he was a really lovable fellow.

There was great excitement when Anthea moved into Queen Charlotte's to have her baby. She produced a beautiful boy – Jamie – and we all appeared proudly on the TV and cinema screens, with pictures in all the papers. The room at the hospital was like Crewe station on a Sunday. We, the family, were all deliriously happy – there had never been a baby like it. Then came the blow. Three weeks later, the little fellow died after what we were told was to be a simple operation. The effect of his death was indescribable to our little family; I am sure my wife never got over the shock. Anyway, a baby girl arrived within the next few months, followed shortly by another boy and this softened the blow considerably. Another little chap appeared on the scene some seven years later (Anthea swears it was an immaculate conception!), so now with Jane, Andrew, and William Arthur, I am the proudest grandad in the country.

At Christmas I was playing *Dick Whittington* at Streatham Hill Theatre and the following year I was at Golders Green Hippodrome in *Cinderella*. How lucky can you get, to be able to stay in London and live at home Christmas after Christmas. And that's not the end of it – I was to have several more pantomimes in London during the following years. A quick look at my diary reminds me that after Golders Green, the order of batting for my pantos was:

1963 *Robin Hood*, Coventry Theatre, with Mike and Bernie Winters and Anton Dolin

1966 *Babes in the Wood*, Wimbledon Theatre, with Roy Castle and Lulu

1969 *Sleeping Beauty*, Wimbledon Theatre, with Roy Hudd

1970 *Cinderella*, Manchester Opera House, with Mary Hopkin, Lonnie Donnigan, Peter Butterworth

1971 *Cinderella*, Theatre Royal, Nottingham, with Dickie Henderson

1972 *Cinderella*, Hippodrome, Birmingham, with Dickie Henderson

1973 *Babes in the Wood*, Richmond Theatre, with Ed Stewart, Lynda Baron.

Ah, you will say, where were you on the missing years? I've kept the best to the last – I wasn't out of work as you suspected. I was at the mighty Palladium, Argyll Street, London, W.1. Please read on.

1964 *Aladdin*, with Cliff Richard, Una Stubbs, The Shadows, Charlie Cairoli

1965 *Babes in the Wood*, with Frank Ifield, Sid James, Kenneth Connor

1967 *Robinson Crusoe*, with Engelbert Humperdinck, Jimmy Logan

1968 *Jack and the Beanstalk* with Jimmy Tarbuck, Jean Bayless, Ivor Emmanuel

I actually only did half the run of the *Robinson Crusoe* panto. On the day we were opening, I asked Albert Knight, the producer, if I could go and get my hair cut as my wigs were not fitting too well. He said, 'Okay, Arthur, you know what it's all about – be here for the opening at seven o'clock.' Well, I visited the hairdresser and, being stage-struck, went straight back to the Palladium where they were still rehearsing the 'chase' scene. My understudy was doing my part very capably, but I had to interfere and do it myself. I ran across the stage, the 'grave' trap-doors opened and I plunged down and cracked all my ribs. They lifted me out gently and an ambulance took me to Charing Cross Hospital where I was X-rayed. They didn't strap me up or anything, just told me the worst. I pleaded with them to give me an injection to ease the pain. I was determined to return to the theatre ('Brave little man carries on') but they said there wasn't a hope. So I spent the evening at home slumped in a chair instead of receiving the acclamation of the Palladium audience with such classic lines as 'I'm the only survivor saved from the wreck.'

Two nights later, I was sitting watching the telly and the pain in my chest seemed to be getting worse. I rang my doctor, who came at once and said 'Heart attack,' and within half an hour I was in the intensive-care unit at St George's Hospital, where I was to spend the next eight weeks.

Lying in a hospital bed gives one time to do a lot of thinking. How bad was my heart condition? Was I ever going to be able to work again? A solicitor friend of mine advised suing the Palladium bosses as they would be covered by insurance. After all, the accident was definitely the fault of the stage-staff. There was some story about everybody having been warned that the trap was 'live', but I certainly was not told. The prospect of getting a large sum of money and retiring to the country was very inviting, but then I thought 'What would I do with myself? Play golf, read, go to the movies, watch television?' It sounded inviting but, having accepted the money, I would never be able to perform again. The 'ham' in me won and I settled for letting them pay my salary for the time I was off. But would I be able to take up where I left off, that was the question. I lay in bed and gave the matter a lot of thought. I had a great many visitors, including Engelbert Humperdinck, who had the nurses swooning all over the place, and an enormous mail. I had some notepaper printed headed 'Maternity Ward, St George's Hospital' and several people whose letters I had replied to wrote to me again c/o The Maternity Ward!

May came to see me only a couple of times. Poor darling, she was becoming very confused and her memory seemed to be going.

This had been obvious for some time and I was terribly worried about it, in fact my doctor said the worry probably contributed to my heart attack. May had become more and more anti-social and hardly left the flat except for a visit to Harrods every afternoon from Monday to Friday. That was her rabbit-run and anything outside that confused her terribly. The doctor said it seemed as if she was suffering from pre-senile decay, which I could not believe. The bright, cheery laughing girl whom I had married, non-drinking, a real home-bird and free from all stresses and strains – how could it happen to *her*?

I left the hospital with strict instructions to take at least a month's holiday. But I sat at home for a few nights and my only thought was, can I go back to work again, or am I finished? After four days I took myself off to the Palladium and walked into my dressing room, where Bill Tasker, my understudy (who had gone on, on the opening night, with no rehearsal and played the part ever since), was putting on the Dame costume for the matinée performance. I told him to 'take 'em off', slapped on some make-up, and put on my drawers, costume, wig and bonnet. I asked the management not to announce the fact that I was playing the part and to leave the notice 'Owing to the indisposition of Arthur Askey . . .' at the box-office and in the programme. I went into the wings feeling 'Well, this is D-Day for me', the music struck up with 'Big-hearted Arthur' and I was on. After a couple of seconds the audience realised it was me, and, well, the reception I received was the best tonic I could have possibly had. I admit to having a tear in my eye as the applause went on and on. I paced myself through the three-hour show and felt none the worse for it. In fact, I felt marvellous in the thought that I could do it. I let Bill Tasker go on for the evening show and the two performances on Saturday, but on the Monday I was back officially and completed the rest of the run – five weeks, twice a day – in the knowledge that Old Man Askey could still keep rolling along, heart attack or not.

Through the sixties I had spent my summers at various seaside resorts. I take it that anyone who is interested – or foolish – enough to buy, borrow or steal this book, will have a slight knowledge of my movements, as faithful 'playmates'. In my earlier days, when doing a summer show at the seaside, we took a house or flat for the season. However, May became disinclined to leave her own home for so many weeks and this necessitated my staying in hotels, as I am useless at looking after myself. I would pass my time pleasantly enough playing golf most mornings with Val Doonican, Bill Tasker, or any of the many pros who are resident at the seaside for the summer. Golf has been a godsend to the profession, and nearly every fully paid-up member of Equity plays it now. In my early days in the business, the average 'pro' rose late, went to the theatre to see if there were any letters, then on to the pub for a drink and perhaps a game of snooker. They would arrive back at the digs late for lunch, have a sleep or go to the cinema, do their stint at the theatre in the evening, sit drinking after the show, then back to the digs, to go through the same routine the following day. Golf changed all this, and I have been lucky enough to have had some marvellous games at the various resorts and at Blackpool in particular, where the members of St Anne's Old Links always made us so welcome.

I always tried to get back to London on a Sunday to spend a few hours with May, leaving, say, Yarmouth at seven in the morning with Val Doonican, spending the day at home and returning the following afternoon. Blackpool was a little more difficult. The late – and great – Arthur Haynes was in one of the other shows there one season and we used to have supper together after the second show on Saturday night, then leave for Preston Station in his car or mine, have a cup of tea with the porters until the Scots Express came in at 2.30 a.m., then into our sleepers, leaving a 6.30 call for the morning. Monday would see us at Euston catching the 12.00 back to Blackpool. We would have lunch on the train and discuss show business in general for the whole journey. Dear Arthur, I can always hear him saying 'Who can we talk about now!'

In 1969 while appearing in Blackpool I had been awarded the O.B.E (ahem) and had to present myself at Buckingham Palace at 10.30 a.m. for the investiture. I didn't fancy the rail journey, nor the rush to get back to Blackpool in time the following day. So I suggested that I waited until the next investiture, but my masters said 'No' – think of the publicity I would be losing. They suggested sending a Rolls to collect me, drive me through the night to London, then back to Blackpool after the ceremony. This didn't enchant me one little bit, so this time, *I* said 'No'. Then they came up with a solution that I fell for – the 2.30 train as usual from Preston, but a private jet to take me back, thanks to Sir Charles Forte.

When I arrived home I tried to persuade May to come to the Palace with me, having tried carefully to explain what it was all about. She said that as the Queen had decided to give me the O.B.E., she should have gone up to Blackpool and presented it to me there! She also asked me what my O.B.E. was for and frankly, I couldn't tell her! She asked what time I had to be at Buckingham Palace and when I said 10.30 a.m., May said, 'I can't get there by 10.30, I've got my work to do. It's all right for the Queen, she's got plenty of help.' So I went with Anthea and her husband and afterwards we had lunch at the Caprice, before I set off for Heathrow and my private plane. A big party had been arranged (without my knowledge) at the Winter Gardens Restaurant at Blackpool that evening. It was a 'reet do' with all the artistes from the various shows and the mayor and other local dignitaries as guests. I suspected that the Tower Company and my masters in London had arranged it all, including the silver tankard which was presented to me. But not so. Our stage manager had organised it, including the printing of the invitation cards, and when it came to the crunch, poor Val Doonican had to foot the bill or we would have all been in jail!

When I returned to London after the highly successful and happy season at Blackpool, I found that May's condition had deteriorated. She would even say to me 'I don't know where my husband is', and on one occasion I had to get Anthea to come over to assure May that I *was* her husband. I had a stream of specialists to the flat, all ostensibly visiting me in view of my heart condition, but they all were unanimous in saying that pre-senile decay had really set in and there was only one thing for it, May must go into a home to be cared for. I naturally hated the idea and suggested I give up work and move to the country with a housekeeper and a nurse, or nurses, to take care of May. They said that was impossible and that I would be in my grave long before May. I took very little work through October and November so as to be with her as much as possible. She made her daily visit to Harrods – she wouldn't let me go with her – and I was always thankful when I heard the key in the front door when she returned. I had to go to Manchester for pantomime and managed to get home for Christmas but could not persuade her to come back to Manchester with me. We had long and lucid conversations on the telephone each evening but I was continually worried throughout the panto.

Spring came and I had to make a decision as to where poor May would have to go. With Anthea, I toured various nursing homes and hated each one more than the last. Eventually we found one which seemed reasonable and accessible and I made the necessary arrangements with our family doctor. May was to be collected by ambulance on the day before my seventieth birthday and taken to the home. I was sick at the thought, as was Anthea, who was very pregnant at the time. On the morning May was to be taken away, I phoned the doctor and told him to cancel all the arrangements. I then phoned Anthea to tell her my decision. She burst into tears and pleaded with me to face up to reality, saying she would lose her baby if things went on the way they were. I phoned the doctor again and told him to let the arrangements stand, kissed May 'goodbye' as she went to have her morning bath, then went across to Anthea's to await the inevitable. Peggy, our faithful daily, phoned to say the doctor and some other gentlemen had called and May had gone off with them quite cheerfully. The rest of the day was a nightmare for me; I phoned the nursing home and was assured that May was all right and sleeping. With the drugs they had given her, I am not surprised. I didn't see her the next day – they asked me not to – but when I did see her the day after, I couldn't believe my eyes. What they had given her I did not know, but I could not credit that such a transformation was possible. She was so bewildered, poor darling, she didn't know anything or recognise anybody. I called every day and her condition worsened – she was obviously drugged all the time. I had hoped there would have been some kind of treatment, but their obvious method was to use drugs to make things easier for themselves.

I started to hunt for another home and found one that was if anything worse, full of old ladies waiting to die. I now began to feel very sorry for myself. All through the years I had given my services and money to various organisations and charities and now, when I wanted help, who could I turn to? Nobody seemed to be able to assist me, or even seemed to care. At last I heard of a wonderful place in Sussex. The health visitor who gave me the information said the place was run by nuns but there was a very long waiting list. I phoned the Reverend Mother and asked if I could call and see her. She said, 'Are you *the* Arthur Askey?' and when I told her I was, she said I could come any time I liked. So I went down the following day to St George's Retreat, a glorious place set in 300 acres in the heart of East Sussex. The Reverend Mother greeted me very warmly, said I was a big favourite with all the sisters and asked me what I wanted. I explained the position to her, first of all saying I was not a Catholic. She said they had all denominations there and religion didn't matter. I told her everything I could about May and how grateful I would be if she could be accepted there as a patient, but I understood there was a long waiting list. Anyway, within two weeks, May was a patient there. For a time she was seriously ill, but with the love and care of those wonderful sisters, she became physically well again and we were able to walk about together in the grounds. My depression eased a lot and I followed my doctor's advice and started working as hard, if not harder, than ever.

I visited St George's whenever possible, at least once a week, and will be ever grateful to the sisters for all they did. I found they were very worldly and fond of the TV, so I took Val Doonican, Vera Lynn, Dickie Henderson, Dora Bryan, Jack Warner, The Bachelors, David Nixon, Cyril Fletcher, Norman Collier, and others down to see them, and they were delighted. We gave them a concert one Sunday afternoon, with most of the above-mentioned in the programme. It was like a Command Performance. With all those stars, somebody had to open the programme, so Jane and Andrew, two of my grandchildren, obliged, and very good they were too. I will never be able to thank my brother and sister artistes enough for their kindness. I thought the nuns were going to make Val a saint and I think some of the sisters almost forgot their vows!

May was in St George's for nearly four years. Eventually her physical state deteriorated and she became bed-bound. As she could not read, knit, sew, watch TV, or listen to the radio, she just sat staring at the wall. I used to talk to her for hours, trying to get through, but it was useless. I would leave her after a visit and find her the next time I called sitting in exactly the same position. But she was in no pain and there was no mistaking how well she was being looked after, which was a great relief to me.

On Sunday, 31 March 1974, I celebrated fifty years in show business to the exact day by topping the bill at the London Palladium. A lot of my mates came on stage at the end of my act and there was a huge cake – candles and all – brought on stage. It was quite a night and Anthea, Bill, my sister Rene, and a couple of friends went out to a celebration supper afterwards. I was feeling very tired: among other chores, I had recorded fifteen programmes for Tyne/Tees TV which necessitated weekly journeys to Newcastle, and this was on top of all my other engagements. Anthea and her family were going on a cruise to the Mediterranean, sailing on 10 April, and she persuaded me to ease up on my work and join them. So on 9 April I recorded my last TV show in Newcastle and boarded the sleeper for London. I arrived at my flat at about 7 a.m. intending to pick up my cases and travel to Southampton to board ship and join the family. The phone rang. It was St George's Retreat telling me that May had died in the night. I didn't tell Anthea (who had seen May the previous day). She thought I had missed the boat, but I went straight down to Sussex to see my late darling wife. She looked like a girl of twenty-one. I phoned Anthea with the news when the ship had sailed, and then set about making the usual morbid funeral arrangements. It was the Wednesday before Good Friday, so nothing could be done until the following Tuesday. The cremation took place very privately near Crawley with just a few close friends and relatives in attendance. So, at the age of seventy-four, my sweetheart from my office days in Liverpool was no more. Her end had been expected for some time, but the blow was just as hard to bear when it happened.

I cannot express how depressed I was when the ceremony was over. I went back to the flat with my sister Rene and just gazed into space. I had no immediate work as I had allowed three weeks for my holiday. I phoned Anthea with all the sad news, then decided I would fly to Athens where the boat was due to call. The family met me at Athens Airport and I found great comfort in being with my daughter and her kids and being able to tell them all the details firsthand. Anthea, of course, had been beside herself and was inclined to reproach me for not telling her before she sailed, but I felt sure I had done the right thing. So ended nearly fifty years of happy married life, except for the latter part, which is still vividly in my mind. I know there are many people in the same position as I was, with relatives who are senile, and my heart goes out to them. To see someone you love in this condition is heartbreaking.

So following doctor's orders and being a natural 'ham', I was soon hard at work again, and still am.

Postscript

MY PUBLISHERS asked me to write 80,000 words and I feel I have already gone over the top. As I have written all this in long-hand in exercise books I seem to have put a million words on paper. Although I am not a writer by profession I hope that my story doesn't take as long to read as it did to write.

Talking of literary matters I have attended many of the Foyles' Literary Luncheons over the last thirty years. I hope in recognition of the many witty speeches I have made that Miss Christina Foyle will put on a bean feast for my book. I recently attended one of these in honour of Tommy Steele. To my complete surprise, the chairman of the lunch, Lord Longford, said on meeting me in the V.I.P. room, 'I hear you said I was a silly old fool.' This was rather a setback, as I was expecting him to say how pleased and honoured he was to meet me. Apparently, I had said this to one of his lady supporters who was persistently asking me to attend one of her crackpot meetings over which Lord Longford presided. So you can't be too careful about what you say when in literary circles. However, Lord Longford did introduce me as 'perhaps the funniest comedian in England'. Perhaps this was a subtle way of getting back at me for calling him a silly old fool. Anyway, I resolved to drop the world 'old' when discussing his Lordship in future.

One luncheon I went to not long ago was far more down to earth. In October 1974 my half-century of work was celebrated by the Variety Club at the Savoy. There were many good friends present and the speeches were marvellous. Max Bygraves and Jimmy Edwards were in top form, Stanley Holloway related our early meeting in Margate, Bill Shankly, the only possible representative of Liverpool, was very pawky, Eric Morecambe remarked, after a typical crack about me, 'I hope Arthur won't mind me saying this – if he does, sod him!', Ernie Wise added 'I am half a double act – Arthur is half a single act,' and Arthur Lowe very succinctly said, 'Ordinary mortals after 50 years are presented with a gold watch, but we are privileged people who carry on till we drop.'

Danny La Rue told me before the luncheon that he couldn't make a speech as it was an emotional occasion. I pooh-poohed the idea, but my speech of thanks was not as jolly as I had intended. The *Daily Mail* in its 'Comment' column, headed 'I thank you', said this:

> Still busy, still buzzing Arthur Askey celebrates fifty years in show business. Behind the over-large glasses there lies something of the sadness of the professional clown. And much of the simplicity too. He's only a little chap, as we all know, but at 74 he manages to look twice as real as many of the pre-packed stars of our TV times. Big-hearted Arthur's half-century of fun-making is worth a cheery salute in these drizzly days.

After fifty years it is still thrilling to receive such good write-ups.

At a function last year I was introduced, with Eric Morecambe, to Prince Charles. He shook hands with Eric and then with me. I said, 'I'm not Ernie Wise, you know, although I have short fat hairy legs.' The Prince replied, 'I know who *you* are. Are you still working?' I said 'But of course,' and he laughed saying, 'I suppose you're one of those fellows who'll probably die in harness!' All I can say, playmates, is – I hope he's right!